Bertha-Size

Your Life

Jane Carroll

Bertha Size Your Life

Book 1 in the Bertha Series

An MKSP Book/May 2014

This is a work of fiction. All names, characters, and incidents are the product of the author's imagination. Any resemblance to real persons, living or dead, is entirely coincidental.

Published by Master Koda Select Publishing, LLC
Copyright © 2014 Jane Carroll

All rights reserved
The right of Jane Carroll to be identified as the author of this work has been asserted by her in accordance with the Copyright, Designs and Patents Act 1988.
Originally published in eBook form by Master Koda Select Publishing. LLC in 2014.

Master Koda Select Publishing functions only as the book publisher and as such, the ultimate design, content, editorial accuracy, and views expressed or implied in this work are those of the author.

No part of this publication may be reproduced, stored in a retrieval system, or transmitted in any way by any means without the prior permission of the copyright holder, except as provided by USA copyright law.

ISBN: 978-0-9905878-9-7

Cover art © Cindy Collins
Cover design © Rebecca White
Interior images © Cindy Collins
Printed in the United States of America

www.masterkodaselectpublishing.com

Dedication

To my beautiful daughters - Jennifer Claire and Sarah Frances who filled my house, emptied my nest, and continue to delight my heart every day.

Thank you.

Acknowledgments

I've always heard that it takes a village to raise a child. This book, my child, is no exception. To each of you villagers I give my heartfelt thanks.

To my mother, Clara Mae Carson, and sisters, Sheila Simms and Cindy Collins, I thank you for your wise words and strong spirits that helped me know anything is possible as long as I remain true to myself. Special thanks to Cindy for giving Bertha a face.

To Arlene O'Neil, I thank you for correcting my words without changing my voice. Special thanks for guiding me through each step of the process.

To my neighbors and friends, Joy Conger and Wanda Beard, I thank you for cooking my food and cutting my grass so that I could devote more time to writing. Special thanks for always appearing delighted as you read and reread the many editions of my work.

To my friends, Laurie and Wayne Gruenloh, I thank you for always being there. Special thanks for giving shelter to me and the manuscript during Hurricane Ivan.

To my former co-workers at South Baldwin Medical Center, I thank you for your support as I left the familiar world of healthcare and entered the unknown world of writing. Special thanks to Candace Miller whose bright smile and "this is really happening!" gave me the courage to continue.

To Reverend Susan Berent, I thank you for assisting me in expanding my belief in God and myself.

To my friend Emmy Scammahorn, I thank you for your willingness to share your professional expertise with me. Special thanks for reminding me that writing is a business and deserves respect as such.

To Grace Moore, I thank you for convincing me before this book was ever started that I have a gift for writing. Without your words of encouragement, these words may have remained forever in my head.

To Jennifer and Sarah, I thank you again for the delight and encouragement you give me every day.

To each of you, too numerous to name, who have shared your stories with me and listened to mine, I thank you for touching my life in such a beautiful way that has inspired me to write these words back to you

Foreword

HELLO Morning Pages. I haven't written since before the wedding. Not much alone time during all the commotion. It went well. She was beautiful. I feel so empty. I suppose this is the true empty-nest feeling. I never really had it before. My whole purpose over these last twenty-three and a half years has been raising my kids. Whatever else was going on in my life, I still had kids to raise. Now they are both totally independent married women and I have the opportunity to redefine myself. I just don't have a clue how to do that. So I write about it, and I go with it, and I grow with it. That is how I deal with it.

I moved into the kitchen to write, moved out of my comfy chair and into the sunshine streaking through the windows. It's cold. I'm cold. This is the Gulf Coast. It shouldn't be so cold. The cat is sitting on the counter behind me sniffing my hair. She is perturbed that I am not in the den so she can push her way into my lap. The sun is dancing on the dog bowl outside. It all looks normal enough. Why does it feel so weird and unsettled?

The sun has left my chosen spot in the kitchen, so the air is cold again. I stepped outside. It is windy and cold. The sun is shining so brightly, but it is deceptive. Many things are. My writing today is not going to the root of my thinking, not touching my soul, dancing across my heart like the sun on the dog's water- just reflecting back.

Is this what it is supposed to feel like? Is this all I have to count for all my years? Two empty bedrooms and a finally silent house? I know I dreamed of this moment for years, but is it really what I wanted? Maybe I'll move. No, I already did that. Maybe I'll cry. No, I already did that, too. Maybe I'll smile. No, my face seems as frozen as the wind. Maybe I'll just wait until tomorrow. What more can I do?

Table of Contents

Getting To Know You 2
Recess 4
Pink Flamingos 8
Sweeping Boundaries 10
Stop 12
Balloons 15
The Snatching 17
Get the Pom-Poms! 19
Like Riding a Bicycle 22
Begonia 24
Long Black Stockings 26
The Killing 28
Lady Liberty 30
Snapshot 32
Budget 35
Ostrich 37
Grandma Minnie Mae's Trinket Box 40
Windows 43
Gardening 44
Mouse Ears 46
Closet Cleaning 47
Sherlock Holmes 49
A Thousand Words 51
Purpose 54
In Bed with the Cat 58
The Hanging 60
Bertha Bits 62
Red Flag 64
Up, Up and Away! 66
Cele-Break 68
Love Letter 72
Derby Girl 74
Stopping Over 78
Ant Bed 80
Gravy 82
Wrong Number 84
Happy "Berthaday" 87
Lottery 92
I Spy 94
Tuned In 96
Monkey Grass 98
Combat 100
Puzzled 103
"Book 'Em Bertha" 106
Bullfrog 108
I Choose 110
Empty Nest 111
Author's Note: 113
Sneak Preview 114

Getting To Know You

Who knew that a simple walk in the park would change my life forever? No, I'm not talking about the positive benefits of exercise and fresh air, although according to the mirror I could use more of both, I'm talking about inviting Bertha to live with me!

I really didn't know Bertha very well. Who had time to get to know her? I had been way too busy being married, twice in fact, and then raising the girls alone had taken a lot of time and energy. And to be honest, I had been in a relationship for the last several years that had consumed every spare moment, and some that weren't spare. Oh, and of course there were lots of hours spent working each week. There just wasn't time to get to know Bertha, too.

But somehow, Bertha always seemed to be on the periphery of my life. I would catch a glimpse of her almost everywhere I went. We'd smile and maybe wave, but we never really had a conversation or anything like that.

Lots of folks politely referred to Bertha as "quirky." True, she was a vibrant red head who was usually dressed in some outlandish outfit involving some combination of lime-green and flamingo pink that most of my friends would never dream of wearing out in public. Bertha was always laughing and in a good mood. She seemed harmless enough. I must admit I rather admired her sense of style.

One day I literally bumped into Bertha in the park. I was walking the dogs and the friendly one went right up to her, pulling me and the shy one along. "I am so sorry. She tends to be overly friendly."

"Oh, that's okay. I don't think you can be too friendly." Bertha reached down to pet the dog and even the shy one allowed her ears to be stroked. Now that was a first! This type of situation usually sent the dogs in two different directions and had me doing my rendition of a human pretzel. This was a nice surprise.

"Why don't you walk with us? I see you all the time, but we've never really talked."

"I'd like that." Bertha took a sip of water from a brightly colored bottle that matched her lime-green spandex bicycle shorts and tangerine tube top.

Almost immediately we were laughing and talking. It seemed that we knew all the same people and had been to a lot of the same places. She had a great sense of humor. I couldn't believe that I had never gotten to know her before then.

It was so easy to talk to Bertha that I soon found myself telling her about my girls getting married and my relationship coming to a close and my job and just all kinds of things. She was a great listener.

Bertha didn't talk about the details of her life very much. She did say that her intention was to enjoy whatever she was doing to the fullest. Then she mentioned that she was thinking about moving to a different apartment but wasn't sure where.

Without even thinking, words started coming out of my mouth. "Bertha, why don't you move in with me? I've got plenty of room with the girls gone and my social calendar seems to be pretty open. The dogs love you. I have a cat. Do you like cats? What do you think?"

Bertha's eyes lit up like fireworks. "That is a great idea! I think we could have a lot of fun. I love your dogs," she exclaimed as she reached down and petted each one, "and I generally get along quite well with cats!"

"Bertha, I apologize. I'm not usually so impulsive. I didn't mean to put you on the spot like that. Would you like time to think about it?"

"Oh, no, I don't need any time. My intuition tells me that this is a fine idea!"

"Then it's settled." I reached out and shook her perfectly manicured hand.

Bertha laughed, "Let the adventure begin."

Recess

Bertha was sitting on the sofa drinking iced tea when I came home from shopping. She was wearing pointy black cat glasses and had her red hair pulled back in a tight little bun thing. She almost looked like a third-grade teacher from the fifties. The lime-green spandex shorts and purple tube top did look more like the Bertha I was familiar with, and they made for quite a contrast. I couldn't help but wonder what was up.

"Bertha, what are you doing?"

"Oh, I'm focusing on the things I want in my life." Bertha took a sip of tea.

"Why are you doing that?" I laid my packages on the table.

"Well," Bertha set down her glass and turned to face me, "focusing on what I want is the only way to get it."

"Really?" I slipped my shoes off and sat in my chair. "I didn't know that."

"Oh sure," Bertha leaned forward. "In fact, I'll show you how it works. What do you want?"

I thought this was a simple enough question and I rattled off my answer. "I don't want to be fat; I don't want to be lonely; I don't want to work with mean, nasty people; I don't want the dogs to dig holes in the yard; I don't want to be in debt; I don't want to work Christmas and holidays anymore; I don't want a hassle about taking time off from work; I don't...."

Bertha held her hand up like a crossing guard and interrupted my answer. "You can stop right there. Do you notice anything interesting about your list?"

I didn't have a clue what she was talking about. I thought it was a great list.

She must have read my look because she continued without waiting for an answer. "You only identified what you don't want in your life. Do you see anything there that is what you *do* want?"

Bertha reached in the corner, pulled out a little soapbox, and climbed aboard. All that was missing was a pointer and she would have done the third grade proud. "Your way of expressing what you want by saying what you don't want is very common. Most people have spent very little time focusing on what they truly want."

She paused and looked down as the cat sniffed the soapbox, even though it had smelled it 30 minutes ago in the corner. It had a whole new scent in the middle of the room. "That is one nosey cat," Bertha commented. The cat laid down nearby, swishing its tail to let Bertha know it did not appreciate being called nosey.

Bertha turned her attention back to me. "Essentially what we think about, focus on, and give our energy to, is what we get. There is a little quirk in the human mind so that we usually overlook the word *don't*. Just think about it. How many times did you tell your kids, 'Don't eat that candy before dinner' or 'Don't be late'? Did it ever seem that they did just the opposite of what you told them? Of course they did. Their sweet ears overlooked the word *don't*."

"So essentially," Bertha pulled herself up a little straighter on the soapbox, "you planted the new thought into their mind. 'Eat that candy before dinner' and 'Be late.' For once, they did e-x-a-c-t-l-y what they heard you tell them!"

I shook my head in amazement. She must have been a fly on the wall during my child raising days! Unlike me, the cat seemed unimpressed with the revelations and left the room.

Bertha made a face at the cat and continued. "Child rearing experts recommend reframing your instructions to your children in order to get the desired results. 'You may have candy after dinner' and 'Be home by 6:00 p.m.' are much more effective statements. Is this making sense?"

I nodded, "Yes."

Bertha smiled and went on with the lesson. "So what have you just said you want? I want to be fat; I want to be lonely; I want to work with mean, nasty people; I want the dogs to dig holes in the yard; I want to be in debt; I want to work Christmas and holidays; I want a hassle about taking time off from work, and whatever else you were about to say when I interrupted you. Now, you know if it works for kids, it will work for you. What do you want?"

"I don't...uh oh...I'm doing it again!"

"That's okay. It takes a little time to change your thinking. It's great that you caught yourself so quickly! Why don't you try again?"

"Bertha, I really want to enjoy my life more. Will you help me do that?"

"Of course I will. What are teachers for?" Bertha laughed and rang an imaginary bell. "Recess!"

Pink Flamingos

Bertha was headed out to the front yard with six pink plastic flamingos under one arm and carrying a little spade in the other.

I must admit I was a bit more than curious as to what she was up to. I was almost afraid to, but who could help but ask when a flock of pink flamingos is on its way out to your front yard?

"Bertha, what are you doing?"

"Oh, I'm going to plant flamingos in the front yard." Bertha tossed me a look that said, "Isn't that obvious?"

"I can see that." Feeling stupid for asking, I continued. "I suppose what I really want to know is *why* you are planting flamingos. You know, there may even be a neighborhood covenant against it."

"Well now, that's a whole 'nother question, isn't it?" Her eyes were dancing. I knew the answer would be a doozy. "Where do flamingos make you think of?"

I pondered a minute and had some image of flamingos and Florida. "South Florida, I suppose," I answered, still confused.

"That's right, I've always wanted to go to Miami. I know if I want to get there I've got to see it, feel it, and touch it." Bertha shifted just a bit to avoid losing her flock. "So I figured surrounding myself with flamingos was a good start. Oh, and I did check the covenants. There isn't one against flamingo flocks."

She looked at the cat who was staring out the window, obviously curious about all those large pink birds that were invading its territory. "You may be one cat over the limit though."

"Good try. You know the cat is well within the pet limit. Anyway, I thought you liked cats."

"I do. We just have a hate-love relationship. You know, the cat hates that I love to live here!"

"Very funny!" I thought for a minute about what she had said. "I have been reading one of your books about Law of Attraction and it does say that it is important to be able to see yourself having the things you want."

The cat must have sensed that it was no longer the topic of conversation because it disappeared into the house.

"That's right. I can't wait to see how it happens!" Bertha was just planting the last flamingo and I thought that would be that. I forgot I was dealing with Bertha!

Next, she dragged a big bag of sand out of the garage and began pouring it around a lawn chair. Then Bertha proceeded to set up a bright sun lamp, aiming it right at the middle of her "beach." As soon as everything was just right, Bertha hurried back into the house.

Quick as a wink she returned, wearing her skimpiest, brightest, purple bikini along with her favorite lime-green straw hat and some pretty wild old-lady pointed sunglasses. She had even smeared sunscreen on her nose. "I love the way it feels to be in Miami!" she said, basking in the bright glow of the sun lamp.

I couldn't believe my eyes. A beach in the front yard? "Bertha, we live at the beach. Why have you set up one here?"

"Well, I did consider just taking the flock down to the beach, but I decided it would be more fun and effective to have them right here where I can look out the window and see them any time."

I didn't have a come back for that, so I just went in the house to check on the cat. Maybe this Law of Attraction could help Bertha and the cat get along better. Something to think about.

Bertha spent several days that week at her beach. Then one morning, she was packing her bags.

"Bertha, where are you going?"

"To Miami of course. I told you Law of Attraction works!" She threw flip flops and sunscreen into a suitcase.

"Bertha, that's great! How did it happen?"

"It's the neatest thing," she announced as she picked up her purple bikini. "The neighbors all chipped in and bought me a trip. I never knew they cared so much."

"Neither did I. This means there's hope for the cat," I mumbled.

Bertha squeezed in a tube top and closed the suitcase. "What are you mumbling about?"

"Oh, nothing. Have fun in Miami."

Sweeping Boundaries

Bertha rushed past me in a blur, broom and dustpan in hand. She was dressed and ready to go to a Mardi Gras ball. I mean we're talking fuchsia strapless sequins with matching three-inch heels and even a matching boa, and there she was, going somewhere in quite a hurry with the broom. I followed as she was obviously too rushed to stop and talk.

When we got to the kitchen, she started to sweep. In no time, she had a little mound of cat litter, dirt tracked in from feeding the dogs, the occasional popcorn kernel, and a stray M&M.

She was sweeping up quite a pile. I couldn't resist any longer. "Bertha, what are you doing?"

"Sweeping."

That's an understatement, I thought. I looked around the kitchen for some new mess that had prompted this unorthodox behavior. "Bertha, why are you sweeping now? You're already dressed for the ball and you look quite beautiful I might add. So why now?"

Bertha stopped briefly and looked at me in sheer disbelief. "Can't you see what has happened here?"

I looked around. It still looked essentially the same as it did an hour ago. "No Bertha, I can't."

Exasperated, Bertha pointed to the pile of stuff she had swept up. "How much dirt do you see here?"

"I don't know. Maybe a cup and a half?"

"That's it!" She pointed to the pile again. "A cup and a half of dirt was on the floor and the limit I can tolerate is one cup. You know how it is when I reach my limit; I take action, no sense fooling around."

I looked down at the pile. "All this for a little trash on the floor?"

"Well now, its trash on the floor. But I normally take action when any of my boundaries are crossed. Don't you?"

"No, now that you mention it, I don't think that I do. Then again, it may be because I don't have many boundaries."

Bertha tried to give me a motherly look, but Mama never dressed like that so it lost something in translation. "Well, it's not too late to set some. You can think about it while I'm gone tonight." She smiled and handed me the dustpan.

I gave her a coy look. "Maybe choosing not to hold the dustpan will be the first boundary I set."

"Good point. I'll sweep fast, just in case!"

Stop

Bertha was sitting on the sofa, big as life, with curlers in her hair. She had on a faded bathrobe and bunny slippers. Not at all the scene I had imagined. We were almost late for our tennis lesson. I had gone into the den expecting Bertha to be in a crisp lime-green tennis skirt, complete with flamingo pink visor and racket in hand, ready to hit the courts, but there she sat.

"Bertha, what are you doing? It's Saturday morning. Time's a wasting." I clapped my hands expectantly. "Let's go! Chop, chop!"

Bertha just sat there watching television and sipping her herbal tea. "You know, we've been doing way too much lately. I'm just going to stop. I'm taking the day off." She glided her arm to the back of the sofa like a queen dismissing a peasant. "Maybe you should, too."

I couldn't believe my ears. "What *doing* too much?" I pointed my finger in the direction of her face. "Haven't you been the one encouraging me to get active, to do something, anything?"

Bertha didn't respond. I caught my breath. "Here I am ready for tennis, then lunch with friends, a class in the afternoon, shopping, dinner out, and then on to the movies. Am I not doing exactly what you have been saying?" I brought my hands up to emphasize the question.

Bertha managed to refrain from rolling her eyes, as she reached in the corner and retrieved that little soapbox of hers. Since I could tell it would be quite a lecture, I sat down in my chair.

"Yes, I must agree that you've gotten active all right. I just think you may have missed the point." At that *point,* the cat looked up at Bertha and fled the room. I couldn't help wishing I could go with it, but I knew I was here for the duration.

"The point of getting active is to have fun. I just don't think you're doing that anymore."

"What are you talking about, Bertha?"

"Well, for starters, let's talk about your week. At last count I believe you had taken six classes, had three friend dates, bought new adhesive things for the bottom of the bathtub, shampooed the dogs, and helped our neighbor paint her den. Not to mention that you worked 50 hours!"

"Yes, I did get quite a lot done." I puffed my chest out a bit… proud of my accomplishments.

Bertha couldn't contain herself any longer and she rolled her eyes. "You know, life is much more enjoyable when lived in balance." She moved her hands up and down like scales for effect. "How many of the things you just mentioned brought you pleasure?"

I squirmed in my chair. "Well…." I squirmed some more. "That's a trick question and I don't have to answer it."

"Just as I thought." Bertha looked as smug as a Cheshire cat. "You're just as out of balance now as you were when the kids were home and you spent all your time focusing on them."

"But Bertha," I was pouting like a six-year-old, "I thought I was doing what you said. I was filling my life. I was getting active."

"Oh no, filling your life doesn't have anything to do with activity. It's more of a feeling kind of thing." She stood on her tip toes in an effort to look like a graceful ballerina, but I don't recall "smushed bunny faces" being one of the positions.

I had to laugh just a little bit.

Bertha's stern look chided me and I settled down as she resumed her normal stance. "Action is only good if you enjoy it."

She looked straight into my eyes. "Now, how much of that stuff did you enjoy?"

I rested my face on my fist and thought for a bit. "You know, I'm not sure I enjoyed any of it. But you know how bad the dogs smelled—that had to be done."

Bertha smiled and stepped down from her perch. "Now what do you really want to do today?"

"I think I'll change out of these clothes and join you for a cup of tea for starters."

Bertha picked up the phone. "I'd like to cancel a tennis reservation…."

Most of the day we just sat on the couch talking about what we wanted to do and how to balance that with some quiet time. We did our nails and ordered pizza. We listened to a meditation tape and got really quiet for a time. I even got out the journal that I hadn't written in forever.

The cat curled up in my lap, evidently enjoying the quiet as much as we were. "Bertha, this has been such a wonderful day. Promise me that you'll stop me more often."

Bertha held up her right hand. "Scouts honor!"

Balloons

Bertha was dressed like a clown. I mean a real clown, with big red floppy shoes and a red rubber nose. She had one of those rainbow-colored wigs on with a hat that was an upside-down flowerpot complete with a silk daisy. Her baggy clown suit was lime-green and flamingo pink striped of course, and she had on a large purple bowtie. She even had on white clown make-up! Bertha was a happy clown with a hot pink smile the size of Texas! She was all set up at the kitchen table, obviously ready for some project involving balloons, a portable helium tank, and magic markers.

So of course I had to ask, "Bertha, what are you doing?"

"Oh, hi." Bertha turned towards me so I could get the full effect of her outfit. "What do you think?"

Bertha's movement woke the cat that was napping nearby. It took one look at Bertha and must have thought she was about to perform a cat juggling act or something because it bolted into the other room.

"At first glance, I tend to be in agreement with the cat," I came a bit closer, "so I'll reserve comment until you tell me what you are doing."

"Okay, fair enough. I am writing desires on these balloons. See how tiny the words are now. Well, I'm filling them with helium so that the desires can get really huge and they can take flight. See? Look at this one. It's my favorite. I've just written 'joy' to mean that I want to feel inner joy. Now let's pump her up and let her soar."

Bertha carefully inserted the helium tip into the balloon and started to pump. The once tiny "joy" started to grow. When the balloon was filled, Bertha painstakingly tied a knot in the end and attached a lime-green ribbon to it. "Come on." She opened the door and took the balloon outside. "Let's see my joy really take off!"

Bertha released the balloon into the air. A small breeze caught "joy" as she floated over our heads and she indeed started to soar. From the look on Bertha's clown face, so did she.

"I know that the more positive thought and attention I give to my desires, the quicker they will soar just like these balloons. Come on, I want to do some more." She clapped her hands like a child and turned toward the door.

When we got back in the house, Bertha busily started filling balloons.

It looked like a lot of fun. "I want to make balloons for my desires, too."

"Do you think you can write your desires without using 'don't'?" Bertha laughed and handed me a bright blue balloon.

"Oh yes, I learned that lesson already!" I picked up the marker and started to write. "Does this meet with your approval?" I held up "passion."

"Ooh-la-la, now you're expressing what you really want! Let's make some more."

In no time, we had a vibrant balloon bouquet ready to soar into the universe. We were giggling like schoolgirls as we released "relationship," "prosperity," "health," "fun at work," and of course, "great shoes." The dogs joined in the fun by chasing the lime-green ribbons as they swept across the yard.

By now, I was getting a pretty clear picture of the balloon process and how it correlated to getting our desires. I just wasn't quite sure why Bertha was dressed like a clown. "I understand about the balloons and giving attention to your desires, but I don't understand why you're dressed like a clown. Is that part of it?"

"Oh this." Bertha laughed as she pulled on her baggy clown suit and did a little curtsey. "Actually, the more fun you have when thinking about your desires, the faster you get them. What could be more fun than being a clown? Besides, I'm going to the park when we're finished here and won't the kids all love it? I'm even going to use the left-over balloons to make balloon flamingos!"

At that, Bertha released the final balloon titled, "delight."

The Snatching

Bertha and I were chattering happily as we strolled casually into the beauty shop. Well, I was casual. She was all dolled up in a bright fuchsia hat with a big flower and a black and white polka dot dress with black and fuchsia heels…quite a sight for our small town!

Suddenly, Bertha stopped dead in her tracks and turned as pale as she could, dressed in that outfit. I veered to the left to avoid a near rear-end collision. "B-e-r-t-h-a, what are you doing?"

"S-h-h-h-h, listen." Bertha's gaze was set straight ahead.

I focused in the direction of her stare. There was Rita, sitting under the big hair dryer, popping gum and filing her nails. She was talking about Bertha with her skinny little friend, Lizzy. I don't know why, but Rita never seemed to like Bertha and she could push Bertha's buttons like nobody's business. In fact, she's the only person I've ever seen get Bertha all riled up. Today was no exception.

Rita must have heard about Bertha's new man because that was her main focus, "Well, he's a bad one that's for sure. Why would a good one want Bertha? She's never had a good one. There's something wrong with her. She just doesn't have a way with men."

Lizzy was just sitting there so little that all you could see was her head nodding in agreement, like that funny little dog on the back dashboard of Mama's car.

I could hardly believe my ears. How dare Rita say such mean, untrue things about Bertha. I didn't know what to do. Thankfully, Bertha did. Quicker than an old maid accepts a marriage proposal, she snatched Rita out from under the hair dryer. Taken aback by the snatching, Rita dropped her nail file and swallowed her gum.

Then Bertha got right in her face, so close she could smell the "Juicy Fruit" Rita just swallowed. "Rita, you aren't in charge here! Nobody died and left you God. It's not your birthday and so, guess what? You're gonna shut that trap up and listen for a change!"

"I am able to attract a great man—the ideal man for me—the one who will love me and share his life with me. I can attract a man who is a balance of funny, quick, sharp, smart, rich, compassionate, generous, loving, romantic, and crazy about me. And what's even better, I already have. In fact, we have a wonderful relationship."

One by one the other hair dryers were turned off as everyone watched and listened to see just what would happen next.

Bertha was undaunted. "Now, you can take that little, and I do mean little, Lizzy and just get out of town! I'm ready and determined to enjoy my life and I don't intend to listen to anymore of your negative talk. Do you understand?"

Rita and Lizzy must have understood because they made a beeline to the front door… leaving a trail of curlers and Dippity-Do in their wake.

Bertha's "audience" cheered. One woman called out, "Bertha, will you talk to my boss for me?" "And my mother?" another added.

Bertha just laughed and sashayed up to the astonished receptionist's desk. "I have an appointment for a manicure and pedicure. I want to look great for my date tonight."

Get the Pom-Poms!

I was tired…that deep down, bone grinding fatigue, that has not so much to do with physical activity as it does with state of mind. My workday was over. I hadn't accomplished much by my way of telling. I just wanted to crawl home and into my nightgown and my nice warm bed.

Mustering up enough energy to open the front door, I was blown away by what I saw. Bertha was squeezing into her high school cheerleading outfit.

The sight of her in a lime-green cheerleading outfit with flamingo pink lettering would have been shocking, even on a good day, and today wasn't one.

"Bertha, what are you doing?"

Bertha sat down to tie her pink and green saddle shoes. "You've been so tired and down in the dumps lately that I decided this is just what you need."

"I do admit that I've been out of it lately and the sight of you in that outfit is amusing." I dropped my stuff on the table and slumped into my favorite chair. "But I really don't see how it is what I need."

"Oh, it's not the outfit that's gonna help, although it is adorable, don't you think?" Bertha didn't wait for an answer, "The outfit is just to get you in the spirit."

"Oh Bertha, now I'm confused. You're going to have to tell me what you're up to." I sighed just a bit.

"It's quite simple." Bertha tugged at the outfit that didn't exactly fit the way it did a few years ago. "People need to be acknowledged everyday in order to feel good emotionally and physically."

"You're preaching to the choir on that one." I pulled my shoulders back in an effort to relax. "The problem is that no one else seems to know that because nobody said one good thing to me today, and I really needed to hear an encouraging word or two."

"That's right." Bertha clapped her hands and grinned, "You're making my next point. You can't always count on other people to acknowledge you, even though sometimes they will. You have to acknowledge yourself everyday for whatever you've accomplished, even baby steps you've taken. There's an easy way to do it, too. I call the whole process, *Bertha-Sizing Your Life!*"

"Bertha what-ing?"

"You know, feeling good is all about raising your energy level. What better way can you think of to do that than to get Bertha-Sized?"

"Bertha, the things you come up with amaze me sometimes. Go ahead and tell me about this Bertha-Sizing."

"It'll be easier to show you." Bertha got up and handed me a pad and pen.

I looked at the paper. On the top left she had written, "What I Did Today." On the top right she had written, "Why That Makes Me Proud."

Bertha waited until I had looked at her handiwork before she went on. "Now I want you to write down three things you accomplished today on the left-hand side."

I sat there for a moment not knowing what to write. Then it started to come to me and I wrote, "Today I tidied my desk at work. Today I stopped for gas on the way home. Today I completed the report that's due in two days."

"Well Bertha, here's my list. I must say they are indeed baby steps."

"That's a great list." Bertha handed it back to me. "Now that's the part anybody could have done for you because they could have observed them. The next step is the best part because only you know why those things made you proud, or made you feel really good. So now, on the right-hand side, write down why you are proud."

I took a few more minutes and thought about each item before I wrote, "Tidying my desk made me proud because I am so much more productive when things are in their proper places, but I don't like to tidy, so it was an effort. I'm proud that I bought gas this afternoon because I tend to procrastinate about those kinds of things, especially when I'm tired. Today I did it anyway. I'm proud that I finished the report today instead of at the last minute because I will have time to review it and be sure that it is perfect before I submit it." Again I shared my list with Bertha.

"See? You are proud of yourself!" Bertha picked up her lime-green and pink pom-poms. She actually started to cheer.

"Two-bits, four-bits, six-bits, a dollar. Everybody who's proud of what they did today, stand up and holler!"

Who would have known I had that jump left in me at the end of this day? Maybe I was getting Bertha-Sized!

"Now," Bertha added, not quite finished with me yet, "what you'll find is that when you really start to acknowledge yourself on a regular basis that other people will too. It's sort of a contagious attitude."

"Bertha, I have just one more question. Until that happens, will you keep the pom-poms handy?"

"Of course," she laughed, giving them one last shake.

Like Riding a Bicycle

The sound of activity in the guest room caught my attention. I went to investigate. There was Bertha, dressed in red flannel footy pajamas, complete with drop seat, assembling the sewing machine. The cat was supervising from the bed. "Bertha, what are you doing?"

"I'm going to make curtains for your bedroom." She barely glanced up from the machine.

"Well, that's a relief. I thought you might be making pajamas for the cat!"

"Very funny. I don't think the cat wants pajamas anyway." The cat was indeed swishing its tail and looking rather unpleasant about the proposition.

"Why are you making curtains?"

Bertha didn't respond. She was lying on her back tightening a bolt under the sewing machine. Those red flannel legs sticking out looked a little like the guy at the quick lube down the street.

I started again. "Bertha?"

Now she slid out from under the machine and shot me that look. You know the one—the one that says you've really crossed the line. "Do you have curtains in your bedroom? I don't think you do. Now that should explain everything."

"But Bertha, obviously you haven't sewn for years. The sewing machine wasn't even put together. What if you've forgotten how?"

Bertha's fire engine red lips curled into a smile (she always matches her lipstick to her pajamas) and said, "I think sewing is like riding a bicycle or having sex—you know what I mean? And besides, how will I find out if I don't try?"

"Okay, Bertha. Have it your way. I'm going to watch TV." I turned to leave the room. The cat jumped off the bed to join me.

"Good," Bertha mumbled, not wanting my help anyway. "But don't take my hairy pin cushion with you!"

The cat bolted past me and disappeared into one of its mysterious hiding places. I started flipping channels looking for something worthwhile to watch, but my heart wasn't really in it. I just kept thinking about what Bertha had said. "How will I find out if I don't try?"

About an hour later Bertha emerged with two lime-green and purple curtains. Just what my bedroom needed to pull it all together. I was so excited that I could hardly contain myself. "Bertha, these are beautiful. You do still remember how to sew. I am so glad that you were brave enough to try."

The cat emerged from its secret place to check out the curtains and to be sure that the coast was clear from pins.

"Oh, it wasn't so brave, just stepping out of the comfort zone a bit. See? Even the cat is willing to do it!"

"I see that," I laughed. "I hadn't thought about it in that way, but when you come right down to it, there are a lot of things in my life that could be like riding a bicycle."

Bertha smiled coyly and headed to the garage with the cat in tow. I'm not sure if she was looking for the bike or a man and I really didn't want to know; the cat on the other hand, was curious.

Begonia

Bertha strolled by in skintight black Levis tucked into turquoise, snakeskin high-heeled cowboy boots and a turquoise western cut shirt with black fringe sewn into the yoke. The shirt was tied at the waist and low-cut. She was showing lots of cleavage. A black ten-gallon hat sporting a turquoise studded, silver band topped off her look. She was carrying a begonia and had her guitar over her shoulder. I had been minding my own business, just reading on the sofa, but the sight of Bertha certainly took my attention away from the mere climax of a murder mystery. "Bertha, what are you doing?"

"Oh, I'm going to sing to my new begonia. I even wrote a song especially for it. Wanna hear it?"

Do I have a choice? I thought, then said, "Of course I would love to hear it, Bertha."

"Well, come on into the kitchen then." Bertha led the way. She gently sat her begonia down on a sunny spot on the counter. The light caught the creamy, off-white to varying shades of coral blossoms ever so nicely.

"Bertha, what gave you the idea to sing to the begonia?" I asked, pulling up a chair for the concert.

"Well, you know that I always want to feel as good as possible." She started adjusting the guitar strings.

"Of course, how could I not know that? But what has that got to do with singing to a begonia? Does that make you feel good?"

Bertha looked up. "Sort of. Actually, I have known for some time that listening to music was a great way to feel good, especially music that reminds you of a time when you were very happy."

"You mean like when I listen to the 'oldies' and I still feel like I'm riding around with my girlfriends in my 1959 VW Beetle?"

"Exactly! It reminds you of a time when you were happy, and for that moment, you feel just as good as you did then."

"That makes sense. But what does it have to do with writing songs to a house plant?"

"Well, I heard on the television that plants do better if you treat them to music, just like people. I started to get a CD for this little jewel, but since I didn't know what kind of music she liked, I decided to really treat her and I wrote her this song."

Bertha swung her guitar off her shoulder and began strumming and singing, "I'll begonia before you get home…I'll begonia before you get home…I'll begonia before you get home…I'll begonia before you get home…I'll begonia before you get home…." Bertha was really belting it out.

I'm not sure if begonia liked her song or not. I knew for sure that it wasn't giving me good vibrations, so I left the room saying, "I'll begonia until you get through!"

Long Black Stockings

Bertha was puttering around the house doing her imitation of housework. She was dressed to the nines as usual. Her long red hair was tied back in a lemon-yellow scarf and she had on the flamingo pink sundress with the yellow flowers. Of course, she was wearing the matching pink high-heeled sandals and nail polish. She seemed so colorful and dressed up for housework.

"Bertha what are you doing?"

"I'm cleaning house of course."

"But why are you so dressed up just to clean? That's one of your favorite dresses. On second thought, why are you cleaning? You hate to clean."

"I know housecleaning isn't my favorite thing to do," Bertha plumped the sofa cushions, "but you know I always want to feel good, and a clean house feels so good."

"I can appreciate that, but why are you all dressed up. Most people wear grungy old clothes to clean house."

"Oh, that's silly." Bertha touched her yellow scarf. "Wearing bright colors and pretty clothes and shoes makes me feel good—makes me happy. Wearing dark, frumpy clothes makes me feel boring and dull—uninspired, even. So if I want to get the house clean, I naturally wear something that lifts my spirits and makes me happy. That makes the job more fun."

Now it seemed that Bertha was on to something. I was curious. "Bertha, what is it with you and bright colors?"

"It started when I was still pretty young. One day I had on a dark dress with black tights and Poppa asked me if I knew what happened to the old woman who wore long black stockings. I said no and he laughed and said, 'Nothing'."

"Poppa didn't want you to wear black tights?"

"Oh, he could care less what color tights I wore. He was just always telling a corny joke of some kind, usually over and over again. But that little joke did get me to thinking and I knew I wanted to go places, do things, have adventures, and have fun. I wanted to live life to the fullest. So even though he was only teasing, I decided to choose bright colors as a symbol to remind me everyday of the kind of life I want. And you know, it really works! Every time I select something to wear that's flamingo pink, lemon-yellow, tantalizing tangerine, lime-green or passionate purple, I get a delicious sense of adventure for the day ahead."

"So bright clothes keep you in a good mood?"

"Not exactly, I just let them be my symbol to remind me that I want to feel good and see life as an adventure."

"I'm afraid that I would ruin my good clothes if I wore them for everyday."

"You're missing the point. You don't have to wear your best clothes to do housework. It's just important to find as many ways as you can to feel good and to enjoy life. One way for me is wearing bright colors and high heels. For you it might be wearing perfume or having a picture of your kids on your desk or something else entirely. It doesn't matter; just choose what works for you. Have fun with it, experiment. Now if you'll pardon me, I'm about to have a vacuuming adventure!"

I decided to put on some perfume and change into something more cheerful before starting my yard work adventure.

I'm not sure if it was the perfume or the outfit, or maybe it was just my intention to enjoy my chores, but I have never had so much fun pulling weeds!

The Killing

I was returning my gardening tools to the garage. The sight of Bertha standing at the work bench, holding a small revolver, shocked me so much that I almost swallowed the shovel.

"Bertha, what are you doing?" I asked in a very calm, matter-of-fact voice. Now was not the time to startle her with the banshee scream that was welling up in my throat.

Bertha turned to face me, still holding the gun.

"Would you mind putting that thing down?" I stayed right where I was.

"Sorry," Bertha laid the gun down on the bench. "I'm just a little nervous. I've never used a gun before."

I took a couple of steps closer, tools in tow. "I know you haven't. So what's up now?"

"I've decided to get rid of Rita and Lizzy."

"You've decided WHAT?" The banshee cry was no longer suppressed.

Bertha recoiled a bit from the sound of my voice. "You know Rita and Lizzy left town after that incident in the beauty shop and I thought that was that."

I nodded and she continued. "Seems as though they are back. Oh, they aren't walking proudly down Main Street at nine o'clock in the morning or anything dignified like that. They are slinking out about eleven o'clock at night down at the Filling Station. You know the place?"

I had heard of it. It was where people went to fill up on beer and stronger after the respectable folks were already in bed, or at least at home.

"So, Rita and Lizzy have been down at the Filling Station running their mouths about me again."

"Bertha, that's terrible. What are they saying now?" I relaxed just a bit and leaned on the shovel.

"It's pretty much the same old stuff, something to the effect that I won't ever amount to much. Rita's still on that kick about my new fellow and Lizzy had the nerve to say that she thought I was just insignificant."

"I can't believe they're still up to that." I shook my head.

"Funny thing is, I hear they are the ones going home alone every night, even with all the construction workers hanging out down there. Who do they think they are?"

She didn't wait for an answer. "Anyway, I figured I had to get rid of them once and for all. That's why I bought this gun and I'm getting ready to use it!" Bertha glanced at the gun on the bench.

I couldn't think of anything intelligent to say, so I sort of shifted my weight and just let her keep talking.

"Rita has intimidated me for years. She's forever telling me what I can't do and why I shouldn't even try. She's always popping that gum. And that voice! No good woman in the south ever sounded like that. Now Rita has teamed up with that little Lizzy. She looks so tiny and frail that you barely even notice her, but when she speaks, it's as loud as any lion's roar."

Suddenly, Bertha burst out laughing. "I can't believe that I have let a hyena and a mouse with a lion's voice intimidate me like this! I'm the one who listens to them. I'm the one who believes them. Everybody else pretty much ignores them. I have lots of friends who treat me with dignity and respect. I'm always getting compliments from other people."

Bertha was still laughing. She laughed so hard she almost split the seams of her tight black capris. Black would have been appropriate to wear for a killing, of course the somberness was offset some by the red and black, polka dot halter top and the red hat and high heels.

Bertha stopped laughing and started taking the gun apart.

Although I really didn't think Bertha could kill anyone, I must say that I was quite relieved that she knew it too. "What are you going to do now?"

"Oh, I'm going to return the gun to the hardware store and get my money back." She pointed to small package on the bench. "I am going to keep the protective earplugs though. They'll come in really handy when I show Rita and Lizzy that they can talk about me all they want to—I just won't listen!"

Lady Liberty

Bertha was sitting on the sofa shaking her head "no" as she flipped through the latest fashion magazine.

"Bertha, what are you doing?"

"I'm looking at the new fall fashions—and I use that term loosely. I mean, who could consider this stuff to be fashion? Look. Here's an article on putting together the perfect wardrobe with just seven mix-n-match pieces. Do you see even one pair of skinny capris? Look at that loafer thing. Who could wear that? It must kill your feet to be all squished in there like that. Navy and gray, what's up with that? Who would wear this stuff?"

I would.

Bertha caught her breath and continued. "Well, actually it probably would be a great wardrobe for some people. That's just it! It would be great for some people, but not everyone and certainly not me. I don't understand why they expect, even desire us to all be alike…to all like the same things, and to all be in the same place. What a boring world it would be if everyone wore the same seven navy and gray mix-n-match pieces everyday."

"You sure are getting awfully worked up over clothes."

"Don't you see, it's way more important than just clothes; it's my right to be whoever I want to be."

Bertha stood up quickly, snatched up that little soapbox from the corner, and climbed aboard. She continued her passionate speech about the freedom in this country, relating how people had given their lives to ensure that we had our rights. She had the Bible in one hand and an American flag in the other and she was really going on and on.

I must admit that I still didn't quite understand the gravity of the situation until her conclusion got my attention.

Bertha was in her bright red and white striped capris and the blue tank top with white stars and the red high-heeled sandals, holding her flag high. She looked a bit like the Statue of Liberty when she proclaimed, "As for me and my house…give me spandex or give me death!"

I was on my way to the garage before she even had time to wave her flag again.

"Where are you going?"

"Since it seems that you've just signed us up for the Revolution, I thought I'd better find a lantern or two to hang in North Church."

Bertha jumped off the soapbox to join me. "Now that's the spirit!"

Snapshot

My black silk dress reflected the mood I was in. I had just finished getting ready for a friend's wedding. I wasn't excited about going. Oh, I was happy for her and everything, but it was just another reminder that I was getting older and was alone again. I did manage to offset the feeling of mourning by wearing Bertha's black rhinestone high-heeled sandals and fixing my hair and make-up just so.

I sat down to watch a little TV until it was time to leave.

Bertha came strolling into the living room carrying her camera and a bag of film. She was dressed in purple from head to toe (yes, including those toes). She had found some purple passion nail polish and had done her nails to set off her purple spandex shorts, halter top and of course, the purple high-heeled sandals. Today, Bertha was wearing a purple beret tilted to the side and with all that red hair cascading down, she looked a bit like a French grape.

I looked up just as Bertha snapped my picture. I covered my face with my hands. "Bertha, what are you doing?"

"I'm taking pictures of you. Say *cheese*." She snapped another picture.

"Oh Bertha, why are you taking these horrible pictures of me? You know I hate having my picture taken. I've gained weight. I don't look the same as I did when I was young and I really don't like being permanently reminded of these facts." I whined like a two-year-old.

Bertha smiled as she lowered the camera for a bit. "I'm taking lots of pictures of you today knowing that when you see them, you will see the beautiful woman that others see when they look at you. When I look at you, I see beautiful eyes that twinkle with a little mischief and a smile that could light up any room. When I look at you, I see the laughter, the warmth and the passion, not the so-called flaws. So what if you don't look like you did when you were young. Who wants to wear diapers at your age anyway?" Bertha climbed up on her soapbox and snapped away from that angle, too.

The more pictures Bertha took the more fun it became. I started posing for them. "Here Bertha, get this one." I crooked my arm around my head and pulled my hair up in what I considered to be a sexy pose. Before I knew it, Bertha had taken three rolls of film and it was time for me to leave for the wedding.

When I got home, Bertha had the pictures developed. What a blast we had looking at them. They were great. They were funny. They were serious. They were even sexy. I loved the one of me standing on Bertha's soapbox holding a flag in one hand and a pink flamingo in the other. There was even a close-up of my feet. Wow! I have sexy feet! I should wear Bertha's shoes more often. I must say when all was said and done it was a wonderful experience. Out of 72 photographs, I actually loved 71 of them and the one of Bertha's thumb really wasn't that bad either.

"Oh Bertha, this was wonderful. I see myself so differently now. How did you know?"

"I knew because feeling beautiful is a choice I make every day. I get to choose whether to focus on my flaws or my terrific features. And you know when I get to choose, I always choose the good stuff. I knew you'd want to, too."

We giggled as we started looking at the photos again.

Budget

Bertha was sitting at the desk pondering over some papers when I came in from work.

"Bertha, what are you doing?"

Bertha looked up to answer, "I'm looking over your new budget like you asked."

I couldn't help but notice that she was wearing her rose-colored reading glasses—perfect for reading budgets, according to Bertha. The glasses did match her adorable pink flamingo sundress, complete with yellow flowers, lime-green leaves and of course her high-heeled sandals. As usual, Bertha was quite a sight.

"That's great. You know I decided it was high time I got my financial affairs in order, so I made a strict budget and I am going to stick to it. What do you think?"

"Well, it seems that you've been very detailed. I mean, here is $30.96 for gas each week and $73.13 for groceries. You've really worked hard to figure things out to the penny."

"Yes, I have," I puffed my chest out proudly. "But you look puzzled. What don't you understand?"

"Oh, I understand it all right," Bertha slid her glasses on top of her head. "It's just that it doesn't leave any room for shoes. What kind of a budget doesn't have room for shoes?"

"I can't say that I considered shoes when I was making my budget. Do you really think it's important to include shoes?"

I could tell Bertha was about to get on her soapbox by the way she looked at me so I sat down for her answer.

"Shoes would the first item on any budget I made. That's because they are very important to me. For you it might be something else entirely. And looking at your feet I'm sure it would be." Bertha looked down and laughed.

"Anyway," Bertha continued, "the point is that the only way you can stick to any kind of a budget, whether it's for time or money or even a diet, is to include room for the things you love. That way, you can be responsible without feeling deprived. In fact, I wouldn't even call it a 'budget.' That already makes it sound like you're giving things up. I would call it a 'Spending Plan' for best utilizing my wealth. Now, what did you leave off your Spending Plan that would make your heart sing?"

I didn't have to think long before I answered, "Flowers, fresh flowers. I love fresh flowers. I'm going to add flowers to my Spending Plan."

I got a pen and calculator, made the necessary adjustments and then handed her the plan back.

Bertha pulled her rose-colored glasses back down on her nose and smiled as she read it over. "Now that's a plan you can live with!"

Ostrich

As I flipped back and forth between Angel Fire and Sugar Loaf, I could see myself cuddled up at the lodge with a cup of hot chocolate and a gorgeous ski instructor named Sven. I was sitting on the sofa luxuriating in the feel of my new baby blue cashmere sweater while looking through the latest travel magazine. I had some time off coming up and had thought that a ski trip would be the perfect holiday. Bertha came into the room just as I was about to get carried away in my fantasy.

The sight of Bertha definitely put an end to the visions of hot tubs and moonlight that were next on my agenda. Bertha had on a lime-green warm up suit with her favorite flamingo pink high-heeled sneakers and was carrying a sand pail and small shovel. I looked at Bertha and then out the window. It was 45 degrees outside and raining. How could Bertha possibly be thinking of going to the beach in this weather?

"Bertha, what are you doing?"

"I'm glad you asked." Bertha ceremoniously sat the pail right down in front of me and pushed the shovel down with her right foot as if she was shoveling up something, then dumping it in the pail.

"I'm trying to find your head." Bertha's face looked much more serious than her appearance.

"Find my head?" I moved my foot to avoid being shoveled. "Whatever do you mean? I'm sitting right here on the sofa enjoying my new sweater and planning my vacation. My head is right here," I pointed to the obvious. "What are you talking about?"

"Well," Bertha propped on the shovel, "I have noticed that you have been spending a lot lately. Mostly you've been charging stuff to your credit cards. I know how much you make and what your fixed expenses such as mortgage and insurance are. When I compare what you are buying with your income, I don't see how you're going to be able to pay off your credit cards. But you just keep spending more like you can't see how much financial trouble you're getting in."

Bertha stopped to take a breath, and then started shoveling again. "That's why I know you must have the Ostrich Syndrome.

I laid the magazine on the sofa. "What are you talking about? What is Ostrich Syndrome?"

"Ostrich Syndrome is when you bury your head in the sand instead of looking directly at your situation. You seem to think that if you ignore your debt, then you won't have to pay it back. You've been acting like that bunny commercial except you just keep spending and spending and spending. I figured somebody had to dig your head out of the sand before you were bankrupt, so here I am—digging."

I couldn't have been more shocked if Bertha had poured a pail of cold water on my head instead of filling one with pretend sand. "But B-e-r-t-h-a," I started to protest and then stopped short. Bertha was absolutely right. I had been spending money that I didn't have, quite often on things that I didn't even need. Suddenly I shivered. The cashmere sweater no longer brought me the comfort it had a few minutes ago.

Bertha was shaking "sand" out of her high-heeled sneaker. "Bertha, you are absolutely right. I have been an ostrich. Do you know that I'm even afraid to look at the balance on my credit card statement each month?"

I hung my head and continued, "I quickly look at the minimum payment and just pay that amount. Well, actually I pay that amount when I can. Sometimes I don't even have the money to pay that part…." My voice trailed off in shame.

Bertha sat down to lace up her sneaker. She seemed to understand that I needed a few moments just to contemplate the magnitude of the insight she had given me. We sat there in a rare silence and I thought.

After a few minutes, I got my courage up a bit. "Bertha, what do I do? I don't know what to do."

"Well, you have done the hardest part already. You have admitted that you have a problem," Bertha replied softly. "Now the fun begins!" she added with that Bertha twinkle in her eyes.

"What fun?" I pulled my knees up under me on the sofa.

"The fun of finding a creative solution to your financial situation of course," Bertha laughed.

"Do you really think my getting out of debt can be fun?" I wrinkled my face in disbelief.

"Of course I do." Bertha climbed up on her soap box. "You know we always want to feel good. Nothing is more important than that we feel good. Now what feels good, being deep in debt or being debt free?"

"When you put it that way, it does sound like it could be okay." I starting to get excited just a bit. "So what do I do first?"

"I've already made you an appointment with a financial counselor." Bertha handed me an appointment card. "I knew you would want to feel good, so I was just one step ahead of you. Your appointment is in an hour. Come on, let's go!"

The appointment with the financial counselor was great. There were so many ways I could manage this debt I had built, and start to live responsibly. She had ideas that I had never even thought of. The whole premise was to change how I treated money and to get a whole new energy flowing in my life. She even gave me some fun money games to play to help change my perspective. Wow! This was going to be fun.

I was almost beaming as I walked back into the waiting room with my new financial plan in hand. Bertha was waiting for me, wearing a lime-green boa around her neck and holding a bright purple one in her outstretched hand.

"What's up with the feathers?"

"Well, you know I've always heard 'if life hands you an ostrich, make a boa!' Here is yours." Bertha laughed as I took mine and proudly draped it around my neck.

Grandma Minnie Mae's Trinket Box

I was coming into the kitchen loaded down with groceries and there sat Bertha at the kitchen table.

She was dressed rather conservatively for Bertha. She had on red capris with a Mediterranean blue button up shirt tied at the waist and a red and white polka dot bandana covered her red hair. She *even* had on white tennis shoes instead of her usual high-heeled sandals. Bertha actually looked like "Rosie the Riveter" the best I could recall. She appeared to be deep in thought and was writing on little slips of paper and putting them into a beautiful jeweled trinket box. I noticed there were also some magazines and scissors lying nearby.

Well I was curious, but I was also about to drop the groceries that I had intended to set on the table. I found a spot for them on the counter. "Bertha, what are you doing?"

"Oh hey," Bertha looked up. "I didn't hear you come in. I was cleaning out a box while you were gone and I found my Grandma Minnie Mae's trinket box. You know I'm named Bertha Mae after her. Anyway, she always had this little trinket box for as long as I could remember, and she would put little slips of paper and other little things in it from time to time."

Bertha held the box up for me to see. "One day when I was about ten years old, I asked her what she was doing and she said she was putting her worries away for safekeeping. I didn't really understand because at ten, I didn't have a lot of worries. Grandma Minnie Mae went on to explain that worrying about things just takes a lot of time and energy away from what you should be doing—living. So she would pray over each worry and then put it away for safekeeping and get on about the business of living. Every few months she would clean it out and take out the worries that were over and pray in gratitude for their being taken care of."

Bertha had a far away look in her eyes as she continued. "Anyway, to make a long story longer, when I found Grandma Minnie Mae's trinket box today, I decided to put my few little worries in it and just let them be."

"Oh Bertha, that's a beautiful story. I'm really touched. Do you mind sharing what you put in the box?"

"Of course I don't. I tell you everything anyway. Why don't you come and sit down here beside me?" Bertha reached over and slid a chair out for me.

I settled in as Bertha started taking the items out one by one.

"Here's a strip of paper about the new fall fashions. You know they just don't make as many capris as I'd like. I cut out this picture of some really cool shoes that I want, too." Bertha glanced down at her feet.

"Would you like to put something in?"

I went in my room and returned with a small picture of my daughters. "I think I'll put the girls in there. I really miss them a lot."

Bertha nodded in understanding. "Oh, and this one is about the wonderful house I found for sale on Paradise Beach that I really, really want."

The cat jumped uninvited onto the table and started sniffing our stuff. Bertha glared at it for interrupting and it glared at Bertha just because it was "the cat." It appeared that they were in a Mexican stand-off of sorts so I decided to continue before war broke out. "Here, I made one for work. We've been really busy and everyone has been pretty stressed."

"Speaking of stressed, here's one about Rita and all the nasty little things she says to me. You know how she can stress me." Bertha turned away from the cat and back to the trinket box.

About that time, the cat started nudging a little piece of paper towards the box with its nose.

Bertha looked distrustfully at the cat. "Now what could this be?"

Bertha picked up the paper and held it up. "Look at this. It says Bertha. What's up with that?"

"I think the cat is doing a pretty good job of telling you something."

Bertha looked directly at the cat. "I don't know how you did that, but I do know that you'd better be worried about me!"

The cat gave Bertha one last glare and nonchalantly started to bathe.

Bertha stuck out her tongue at the cat. "Act like you're not scared, I don't care."

I decided it was time to change this relationship. I picked up a piece of paper and started to write.

Windows

The house was cold when I came home. I looked around and noticed that all the windows were open. The curtains were alternately puffing out and sucking back in. They looked sort of like the face a goldfish makes. It would have been pleasant enough except for the temperature.

Bertha came in from her room wearing a turquoise warm up suit and matching turquoise running shoes. I doubted seriously that she had been running and it was a far cry from her usual capris and high-heels.

"Bertha, what are you doing?"

"Oh, I'm opening windows." She flipped that red hair back, letting me see that she thought the answer was obvious.

"Well Bertha, I can tell you have opened all the windows." I shivered and rubbed down goose bumps. "What I really want to know is why you have all the windows open."

"Oh well, that's simple."

But I knew with Bertha it never was.

"I'm practicing allowing. I figured the best way to let the things I want come into my life is to open the windows and just let them in." Bertha did a generous sweeping motion with her arms.

"I'm not sure I understand." I reached for a lime-green velour throw.

"Well, I have set forth my intention that everything I need will become available to me. I know that sounds simple, but sometimes it's not. Sometimes, after I have become really clear on what it might be that I'll need, I start focusing more and more on how it could actually happen. I find that by the time I've started thinking like that, I'm so uptight that I'm resisting instead of allowing. So I opened all the windows to remind myself of how easily everything I need can flow into my life." Bertha shivered as she spoke.

"Oh, Bertha, that's a great idea. Will it work for me too? Can everything I need become available to me?" I asked excitedly.

"Of course it can. It already is."

At just that moment, the heat kicked in. "Wow, that is precisely what I needed. Bertha, you are right as usual. What else can I allow?"

"It's up to you. The sky's the limit!"

Gardening

I was sound asleep when Bertha burst into my room. She flung open the curtains and pulled back the covers.

"Bertha, what are you doing?"

"Time to get out of bed!"

"I don't want to." I tried to pull the covers back up, but Bertha was holding on tight and they didn't budge.

"Why should I get up anyway? I'm not needed anymore. The kids are grown. I'm single. Nobody wants me."

"You sound like you're about to sing the worm song," laughed Bertha. "You know the one. 'Nobody loves me, everybody hates me, I'm going out in the garden to eat worms.' Now come on, we *are* going out in the garden."

Suddenly I was quite awake.

"But Bertha," I pleaded, "I don't want to eat worms. It'll make me vomit. Please don't make me."

"Oh, you're silly. Of course we aren't going to eat worms! We're just going to garden."

I noticed that Bertha was indeed dressed for gardening. She had on her lavender leather gardening gloves and matching hat and sneakers. She was very coordinated with a lavender print jump suit. I must say she looked adorable. And boy was I relieved that I didn't have to eat worms! With Bertha, I'm never quite sure what will happen.

"Bertha, why are you getting me up to garden so early on Saturday morning?" Even half asleep I could tell that Bertha wasn't going away, so I started to crawl on out of the bed.

"Well, you've been pretty down lately." Bertha started tidying the covers as soon as my feet found the floor. "And I got to thinking that Mama used to always say that working in the dirt was a sure fired cure for the mully-grubs," Bertha proudly stated.

"Now, I'm not exactly sure what mully-grubs are, but I think you have them. So I thought we'd go out and garden. We'll spend some time in the sunshine and fresh air and get dirt on our gloves."

"I thought it was supposed to be to get our hands in the dirt."

"Hardly. I just had my nails done." Bertha wiggled her lavender-splavender manicure for effect. "Come on. Let's go."

Soon, we were out pulling weeds and planting zinnias and marigolds. Despite my grumpy start, I found myself smiling and enjoying the way the sun felt on my face. And I loved watching the dogs. They were alternating playing tug of war and lazing in the sunshine.

"I wonder if we can train them to dig up weeds." Bertha looked at the dogs and pointed to an unwanted green patch. "Weeds. Dig!"

The dogs gave Bertha a funny look and dug up a marigold.

"To answer your question, I'd say it is doubtful, but feel free to keep trying!" We had a good laugh as Bertha replanted 'Goldie.'

We spent most of the day in the garden and I was having such a good time that I never did see the first mully-grub.

However, Bertha did find an earth worm. "Do you want to try it?"

"I think I'll let you have the first one!"

Mouse Ears

I was surprised when I went into Bertha's room to distribute clean towels. There she stood, packing her suitcase. I didn't know she was going on a trip, but she's pretty spontaneous so that didn't surprise me. She was dressed in her favorite purple spandex shorts with the flamingo pink halter-top and the matching high-heeled sandals and that certainly was normal for her. So why was I surprised? She had on Mickey Mouse Ears, and even for Bertha, that was different!

"Bertha, what are you doing?

"I'm packing for a trip to Orlando. I'm going to Disney World."

"I guess that explains the ears. But you haven't even left yet, why are you already wearing them?" Expecting a long answer, I sat down in the chair.

Bertha turned around and her eyes were twinkling. "I've been thinking that most people wait until they get there to start having fun and acting like a kid. That seems like such a waste of a 12-hour trip. Well, I decided why not enjoy the journey, too? That's why I'm wearing my mouse ears to Disney instead of waiting until I come home!"

Bertha pulled out her little soapbox and climbed on. I was curious as to what it was doing under the bed. I decided not to ask. Some things are better left unknown.

"It's a lot like life. Too many people are waiting for something to happen in their lives before they start to enjoy what they have. How many of us are waiting to lose weight, get married, have kids, get a better job, have money, turn 21, get a sports car—the list could go on and on, instead of just enjoying everything they have today?"

"Bertha, you really are on to something. I know I have been guilty of that myself." I wondered if she had any extra Mickey Mouse Ears hiding in her suitcase I might just "enjoy" wearing them at home this weekend.

Bertha must have read my mind. She stepped down, reached in her bag, and handed me the desired Mickey Mouse Ears. "You got it, sister!"

Closet Cleaning

Quickly awakened and still in shock, I caught a glimpse of Bertha dressed in purple spandex shorts and a red bandana in the midst of cleaning my closet. She had things flying in every direction.

It would be nice to say that I calmly asked her what she was doing. The truth is, it was six o'clock on a Saturday morning. I let out a scream that would wake the dead.

"Bertha, what are you doing?"

"Hold on. Don't get your panties in a wad." She flung a stray pair across the room for effect.

"You've been complaining lately that life seems a little stale. I've even noticed that the good things aren't coming to us like they once did." Bertha dumped out a box of perfectly good stuff on the floor and started sorting most of it into the garbage can.

Bertha picked up my favorite scuffed tennis shoes and flung them into the can. "Money seems to be tighter. We just aren't having a lot of fun either."

I rubbed my eyes. I was not amused. "What has that got to do with your unsolicited attack on my closet, not to mention my favorite shoes?"

"Well, Grandma Minnie Mae used to say that when life seems to be closing in on you that it must be time to make more room." The contents of another box found their way to the garbage.

"And I would hardly call those things shoes." Bertha looked down at her racy, high-heeled sandals. "Now *these* are shoes!"

My mouth opened in protest, but no words came out. Unlike Bertha, I was speechless.

Bertha left the room and returned with another garbage can. She was taking this concept of making room for life very seriously.

"Bertha, do you think this will help make things better?" I propped up on one elbow so I could see her.

"I've seen it happen. I had a friend who was miserable in a dead-end relationship. She met the greatest guy almost the exact minute she decided to call it quits. And remember when you got serious about changing jobs, you noticed the perfect job posted at your same company?" Bertha wrinkled her nose at a pair of knotted up panty hose and did her rendition of a hook shot into the can.

"You're right about my job. That was the neatest thing. Does it really work all the time?" I climbed out of bed to rescue my tennis shoes—no point in getting carried away.

"Yes, it does. There's a scientific principle that nature abhors a vacuum." Bertha surveyed her progress and smiled. "Every time something gets empty, something has to come along to fill it up."

I looked down at the ratty tennis shoes I had rescued. "I think I will let these go and see what takes their place."

Bertha ceremoniously held the can for my shoe deposit. About that time, the cat came strolling in to check out the commotion. Bertha looked at the can and then at the cat.

The cat crept over to me; it must have read Bertha's thoughts. "I wouldn't if I were you. You know nature might just send you two cats to take its place."

"No fair. You're using my lesson against me."

"Only because you're such a good teacher! Besides, I like the cat." I joined the cat in a Cheshire smile.

Sherlock Holmes

I couldn't imagine what was going on when I walked into the den. There was a chair turned upside down. Open books were scattered across the floor. A picture was even off the wall. Bertha was right in the midst of things with this huge magnifying glass looking under the sofa cushions.

Now granted, that in and of itself is pretty odd, but you should have seen Bertha. She was dressed as quite the sleuth. In fact with that hat and trench coat, she could have been with Scotland Yard except that I never saw Sherlock Holmes dressed in tantalizing tangerine the way Bertha was. Yes, everything that Bertha wore from head to toe, including heels, matching nail polish and lipstick was tangerine.

I must admit I was curious and even though I am often leery, I asked that famous question, "Bertha, what are you doing?"

Bertha turned towards me still holding the magnifying glass close to her face. She looked a little like a third grader in science class with that giant eye on one side.

"Be careful. Don't touch anything. I'm looking for clues." Bertha looked as serious as she could dressed like that.

"Bertha, what clues? Has there been a crime? Where's the cat? Have the dogs been in the house? Where are my pearls?" My voice rose with each question.

"Calm down, silly. There hasn't been a crime. The cat is fine. The dogs are outside and I'm wearing your pearls for safe keeping, just in case." Bertha touched her neck reassuringly.

"You know we've been practicing Law of Attraction for a while now and we've been reading some great books. Now, I'm looking for clues that change is actually taking place in our lives." Bertha aimed the magnifying glass under another cushion.

"Well, I for one have noticed a lot of changes. I'm happier most of the time, I'm learning to focus on the things that I want, I don't have the mully-grubs anymore, and lots of wonderful new things are coming into my life. Is that the kind of thing you are talking about?"

"Yes, that's it exactly." Bertha's eyes sparkled as she nodded her head.

"Then why," I pointed at the couch, "are you looking under the sofa cushions?"

"Well," Bertha grinned, "where else would you look for change?"

A Thousand Words

I stomped in from work and slammed the door behind me. The noise startled Bertha, who was sitting at the table painting her nails 'Hot Rod Mama' to match the new Capris and tank top she had on. Of course her high-heeled sandals matched, and she had already finished her toenails. Oh, she looked hotter than I felt, and I was steaming!

Bertha's expression as she looked up, showed that she was about to ask me what was wrong, so I saved her the trouble and just started right in. "You won't believe that girl at work. You know the one I told you about who's really smart and needs to go back to school so she can get a higher paying job like she deserves. Today I tried to point out all the reasons why she should go to school. I don't think she really even listened to me. She just smiled politely, thanked me for my concern, and went on about her business like I didn't know what's best for her. I've talked to her 'til I'm blue in the face. What else can I do?"

"Well, for starters, you can leave her alone." Bertha blew on her nails to speed up the drying process.

"What? Leave her alone? Watch her waste her life in a dead-end career when she has potential?" I fired off in disbelief.

"We've had this conversation before," Bertha paused to blow on her pinkie, "if she hasn't asked for advice then you really can't give it to her. Besides, it's hard enough to know what's best for yourself let alone anyone else."

"That may be true—but you just don't know this girl. She really has potential," I whined.

Bertha got up from the table and left the room. She returned carrying an old photo album, very carefully so as not to mess up her nails. This seemed like an odd time to reminisce. I had a point to prove. "Bertha, what are you doing?"

"Grandma Minnie Mae always said, 'A picture is worth a thousand words' so I thought I'd show you this picture, since I don't have time for a thousand words. I have a date tonight and I don't want to be late," Bertha grinned.

I still didn't understand, but I sat down next to Bertha as she flipped through the pages of her life. There were all sorts of pictures of her and her family on picnics and outings. There was a nice picture of

Bertha and her sisters in front of the dogwood trees on Easter Sunday. Obviously, none of these pictures spoke because she kept turning. She stopped when she came to one labeled 'Christmas 1965,' and screamed, "this is it!"

"This is what? It's just a picture of a bunch of your family standing in front of a Christmas tree."

"Oh, it's much more than that," Bertha's eyes twinkled. "It's the thousand words!"

"Okay, I'm game. Why is this picture worth a thousand words?" I asked skeptically.

"Let me give you a little history," Bertha started. "This was the Christmas that Grandpa Charlie was so sick. Grandma Minnie Mae couldn't take care of him 24 hours a day and Mama and her brothers had to work, so they hired this man—the one right here in the center of the picture—to live there and take care of Grandpa Charlie at night. So of course, we included him in our Christmas celebration that year."

"Well that's nice, but if you don't get to the point of the picture, you're gonna use all your words up anyway and be late for your date," I replied in response to her history lesson.

"Okay, let's get to it. Do you notice anything odd about the hired man?" Bertha pointed a "Hot Rod Mama" at the picture.

I looked at the picture for a few seconds before it hit me. "He's not wearing any socks and it's the dead of winter! Poor man probably couldn't afford socks. But what has that got to do with me?"

"Okay, so now that you've got the picture, I'll explain. It was a cold winter and just as you pointed out, he didn't have on any socks. He never wore socks. We all felt really bad for him because we knew his feet must be cold. He was a nice man, so of course we all wanted to help him in any way we could." Bertha paused to let that much sink in, then continued, "so without even discussing it, everybody in the family bought him socks for Christmas. There were brown socks, blue socks, black socks, and even white socks. He probably could have worn a different pair of socks every day for a month."

"I bet he was really happy," I interrupted, wiggling my toes as I spoke.

"Well, he thanked us all and seemed just as pleased as punch." Bertha flipped the page to the next picture labeled, "New Year's Day 1966." "Notice anything about this picture?" Bertha smiled knowingly.

"He doesn't have on any socks!"

"That's right." Bertha laughed. "He never wore the first pair of them. Seems he didn't like to wear socks. He was happy just the way he was."

"Oh Bertha, those pictures *were* worth a thousand words. I think I'd better 'stick a sock in it' when it comes to giving unwanted advice."

"Grandma Minnie Mae couldn't have said it better herself." Bertha laughed as she put the pictures away and answered the door for her date.

Purpose

Bertha was in her pajamas, although I didn't know why. She hadn't slept in two nights. Oh, she had gone through the motions of going to bed. She coated her face with cold cream and smeared her makeup all around, then wiped it off with a Kleenex. She put her hair up in those curlers she wore sometimes. Bertha brushed her teeth and said her prayers, but the sleep didn't follow. It was more like, "Now I lay me down to toss and turn and be miserable all night long." What was up with Bertha?

Rita had been by to visit. She came under the pretense of "Bertha's own good," a sure-fire way of saying, "I'm gonna stab you in the back with this dagger and turn it just a bit," or at least that had been my experience with people. Rita didn't prove me wrong, either.

Seems as though the biggest department store in town was looking for a shoe model for the new fall line and Bertha was sure the job was hers. She knew shoes. Bertha had great feet. They were sexy feet by most accounts. She always kept them looking buff with a perfect pedicure. Knowing the job was hers, she set her intention. "I want to be the shoe model." Closing her eyes, Bertha saw herself in the new styles, saw her picture being taken for the catalogs and newspaper ads. This was hers.

Then Rita showed up. Rita's cousin was on the committee to select the shoe model and had told Rita all about it. Now, she felt it was her duty to inform Bertha that the committee was interviewing other applicants. In fact, they were seriously considering one in particular, someone from another town. Rita didn't really know her, but she had heard that this woman had flat arches and round heels. Anyway, Rita didn't want Bertha to be disappointed and thought maybe she shouldn't get her hopes up about the job.

Rita left smirking under her breath. She knew she had planted a seed of doubt in Bertha's mind that was bound to sprout and take root quicker than a dandelion in a freshly weeded garden. The plan had worked perfectly, too. Bertha immediately looked down, noticed that the polish on her little toe had chipped, and began to wonder if they might really choose this "out-of-towner." Maybe this wasn't her job after all. Maybe she didn't know as much about shoes as she thought. Maybe this other woman was the shoe expert of all times. Maybe her feet were more beautiful than Bertha's. Or even worse, what if she really had ugly feet and knew nothing about shoes? Oh, that *would* be even worse!

So now, Bertha was sitting at the kitchen table in her lime-green polka dot pajamas with the matching fuzzy frog slippers. The aroma of her freshly brewed coffee had lured me out of bed and down the hall. Bertha had both elbows planted firmly on the table and was holding her coffee cup about halfway to her face. She was staring out into the distance like Mama always did when she was deep in thought.

"Bertha, what are you doing?" I poured myself a cup of wake-me-up.

"I was just thinking about the shoe model job." She continued to stare into space. "You know, I've been so stressed about this job and the possibility of someone else getting it that I haven't even been sleeping. So last night as I tossed and turned, I decided to do a meditation to find out my life's purpose and I figured it out."

"Oh Bertha, that's wonderful," I sat down and blew on my coffee to cool it a bit. "What is your life's purpose?"

Bertha took a sip of coffee. "My life's purpose is to inspire women to wear heels. I suppose I've always known it on some level. I just wasn't fully aware of it until now."

"Bertha, you must be right. That certainly sounds like you."

"I know," Bertha put her cup down, "that's why I've been so uptight about this shoe model job. It is right in line with my life's purpose. Just think of all the women I could inspire. Women everywhere would be in heels. I just have to be the shoe model...." Bertha's words sort of trailed off and she was once again staring into space.

I thought it best to leave her with her thoughts, so I went about the business of getting ready for work.

When I returned that evening, Bertha seemed more like her old self. She was dressed to the nines in her favorite red sundress with the matching heels. She had gone for a fresh manicure and pedicure and the "red hot chili pepper" polish matched perfectly. Her red hair was freshly done. She looked stunning.

"Bertha, you look beautiful. Did you get the job? Are we celebrating?"

Bertha turned and smiled. "I haven't heard anything else about the job."

"Oh, then why do you look like you're ready for a celebration?" I tilted my head to the side.

Bertha brushed her hand down her skirt. "I've really thought a lot about my life's purpose today and even did some more meditating about it. You know, I realized that there are many ways to fulfill your purpose. If there were only one way, it would be called your 'life's project' now wouldn't it?"

I had to admit she had made a great point. "Bertha, I never thought of it that way. So why are you all dressed up? What are you going to do?"

"Well, I got to thinking that since there's always more than one way to skin a cat, that I'd just figure out another way...."

Bertha's reply was interrupted by the cat bolting from the room. Evidentially the cat remembered the unfortunate incident involving Bertha, its tail and the vacuum cleaner, and wasn't taking any chances today.

"Your cat is weird," Bertha pointed her finger at me, as if I could control the cat.

"You're the one who attacked it with the vacuum last week. It probably thinks you're the weird one!"

"You know that was an accident. I told it I was sorry. It doesn't have any sense of humor at all. Anyway, tonight we're celebrating that life is full of possibilities and that I am open to multiple opportunities to fulfill my life's purpose. The shoe model job may or may not be one of them. In fact, I'm considering writing a book about shoes. What do you think?"

"Bertha, that is a perfect idea. There's no telling how many women you can inspire with a book. You've inspired me already." I looked down at the racy little sandals I had worn to work. "Remember the clunky shoes I used to wear?"

"I'd rather not. Thinking of them might make me have nightmares and I want to get some sleep tonight!"

Just then, the phone rang. Bertha went to get it in the other room. She was almost floating when she returned. "You are looking at the new fall shoe model. Can you believe it? I get to be the shoe model and I'm going to write a book. Just think, I have Rita to thank for all of this."

"Rita? Why Rita? Rita was mean and nasty to you and tried to make you doubt yourself. Why would you owe anything to her?" I couldn't believe my ears.

"If Rita hadn't made me doubt myself, then I wouldn't have discovered my life's purpose, and even though I still would have gotten the shoe model job, I wouldn't have decided to write a book about shoes. So the joke's really on Rita, isn't it?" laughed Bertha.

"Now come on. Let's go celebrate."

In Bed with the Cat

It was early and I had decided to get a jump-start on some housework. As I walked by Bertha's room, I saw that she was already up and making her bed. She still had on her favorite red footy pajamas with the drop seat. Of course, she had on matching red lipstick. That's just Bertha.

It all sounds normal enough, except with Bertha, nothing is ever normal!

I noticed that the cat was laying on the bed big as you please and refused to get off. Bertha fluffed and smoothed the blanket while the cat just laid there like dead weight... staring at her.

Bertha must have thought she was in charge. She tugged at the blanket again in an attempt to make the cat airborne. Now the cat was glaring, but it didn't move.

Bertha pulled the flamingo print bedspread up over the cat. The cat usually hated to be under the covers, *except* for this time. She waited a few moments, looking expectantly at the small lump, but nothing happened.

I couldn't stand it anymore. "Bertha, what are you doing?"

"Well I'm making the bed of course."

"I can see that. Did you happen to notice the cat is in the bed?" I pointed at the obvious.

"Duh," Bertha replied, a little out of breath from the struggle. "Of course I noticed the cat is in the bed. I just can't quite seem to get rid of it this morning." She flipped her hand in the cat's direction. It didn't shoo.

"I think I'll put my money on the cat winning this one. Why don't you just leave the bed unmade?"

"Oh, I suppose I could do that." Bertha turned to face me briefly. "But I'm going out and you know I hate to come home to a messy bed. Anyway, the struggle reminded me of dealing with fear."

"How in the world does the cat refusing to get off the bed remind you of fear? You may be afraid of it, but I don't think it's exactly shaking in its puss-n-boots over you."

"Of course I'm not afraid of the cat." Bertha poked at the lump in the bed to no avail. "It's an analogy."

"Okay, if you say so. Do you want to explain?"

"Gladly." Bertha whipped out that soapbox of hers quicker than a hungry girl scout could eat a s'more and climbed aboard. "Have you ever had a time in your life when you really wanted to do something, but fear plopped down in your way like the cat just did?"

"Quite a few actually. Do you want me to list them chronologically or alphabetically?"

"I'm in a hurry so I'll take your word for it." Bertha looked down at the bed with its unwelcome lump and shook her head.

"The important thing is how you dealt with the fear. Did you let it immobilize you or did you keep on trucking?"

"I hadn't thought about it, but lately I seem to be doing a lot more trucking."

"I know. I'm expecting you to start hanging out at the Truck Stop soon."

Bertha jumped off the soapbox to avoid the pillow I tossed.

"I figured it was the same thing this morning. I could either leave the bed messy feeling defeated by the cat, or I could ignore the cat and make the bed anyway. I really wanted the bed made, so that felt better."

"I know, you always choose what feels best. So the bed has to be made. What about the cat?"

Bertha reached under the bedspread, removed the cat and returned it to the foot of the bed.

About an hour later, Bertha came in the den looking gorgeous. She had the confident look of someone who had just conquered a cat.

"Have a gre…." My well wishes were interrupted by the thud of the cat jumping off the bed. Bertha and I looked at each other and laughed as the cat took a victory lap around the den.

The Hanging

I looked up from paying bills just as Bertha walked by carrying a hammer and a nail. "Bertha, what are you doing?" I asked still holding the pen in my hand.

Bertha looked in my direction. "I'm getting ready for the hanging."

I was shocked and concerned. "What do you mean hanging, Bertha? They don't still hang people in this country, and even if they did, you shouldn't go to one. Besides that, why are you taking a hammer and nail? Are you working on the gallows? Where's the cat? You aren't still mad at the cat, are you?"

"Oh calm down." Bertha ran her fingers through all that long red hair. Her nails were painted the perfect shade of "Street Riot Red" to match her red sundress and high-heeled sandals. She really looked quite beautiful to be going to a hanging.

"It's not that kind of hanging. The cat is fine. Even though there is always a reason to be mad at it, I'm not building gallows to hang it. There's no kangaroo court taking place in the back yard. I'm just hanging the artwork I bought last night."

Boy did I breathe a sigh of relief, and so did the cat. I laid my pen on the table. The cat slinked into the other room, just in case. "I didn't know you were looking for artwork."

"I wasn't, but…here, hold this a minute."

I took the extended hammer and nail. Bertha grabbed the soapbox out of the corner. I thought she might be going to use it for a ladder, but no, she climbed right on and started to talk.

"You know that in order to attract good things into our lives we have to feel good. Our mood is like a magnet. If it is turned the right way, it attracts what we want, but if it's turned the other way, then it pushes them away."

I smiled. "Seems like you've mentioned that a few thousand times. What's that got to do with buying a picture?"

"Everything. I was out shopping for shoes, minding my own business, when I saw a painting in a gift shop window. It was of a Mediterranean terrace overlooking a body of water. I was immediately transported to Lake Como, Italy. I could see myself sitting there having breakfast and overlooking the lake. It was so real that I could smell coffee and freshly baked bread." Bertha took a deep breath as if to savor the aroma one more time.

"Let me guess. Since it gave you such a wonderful feeling to see the picture you decided to bring it home. Now you can take a virtual trip there anytime you want and feel good in the process." Bertha's face was so radiant I could almost see her "good vibrations."

"That's exactly what happened! You're getting so smart."

"Thanks for noticing. You know, I was a little down paying the bills, but I feel better just hearing you talk about the painting. I can't wait to actually see the picture."

Bertha hopped off the soapbox and took her tools. "We'll fix that in a jiffy. Here, hold the nail."

Bertha Bits

It was early. The sun was just starting to wake up and so was I. Staggering to the front porch, I was just wanting to enjoy my first cup of coffee in the cool, calm sunrise before I faced my day.

As I opened the door, I was startled by Bertha sitting on the porch swing. I know she usually prefers to sleep through sunrise unless something really important is going on. So I was curious. "Bertha, what are you doing?"

Even though I ask that exact same question hundreds of times a day, I am usually taken aback by the answer. Today was no exception.

"I'm just thinking," Bertha replied rather wistfully. It would have felt like an almost tender moment except that the picture of Bertha and the words seemed to be such a contrast. Bertha had on her zebra print pajamas complete with matching fuzzy slippers, and had her hair in those huge rollers that most of us gave up in the sixties when hot rollers became popular. There was even an orange juice can right in the crown of her head. I had wondered what possessed her to make orange juice last week and now I knew. Bertha had on her black pointed reading glasses with the rhinestones. She was holding a zebra print journal in her lap and matching pen in her hand. Not quite think tank attire. At least one could say Bertha was well coordinated. It just seemed out of character for her. I had to probe further.

"Bertha, what are you thinking about so early in the morning?"

"Well, if you must know, and I know you must, I'm working on my book. You know the one I'm writing to inspire women to wear heels."

"Bertha that's great. You are so inspirational and have so much wisdom. You have such a style, a flair even. I bet your writing is incredible. I can't wait to read it. Let me see what you've written so far."

Bertha held up the journal so I could see. It didn't matter that I didn't have on my reading glasses because there were no words, only a blank, glaringly, white page.

"I never knew it could be so hard. I thought writing would be as easy as thinking and I think all the time. I have beautiful, even brilliant thoughts. It's just that when I opened this journal and saw all this white space, all those thoughts tuck-tailed and ran. Now I'm left here all by myself with this blank journal. What do I do now?"

This was a first—Bertha asking *me* for advice. I considered my words carefully before I spoke, remembering the advice Bertha had given me in similar situations. "You know Bertha, *maybe* we could just talk about what you want to say, and that might help you get started."

Bertha started telling me the ideas she had for her book. As she talked, she seemed to coax her "scaredy thoughts" and they started to appear in black and white. It was almost like watching one of those old Polaroid pictures develop. First, one or two words came and then a paragraph followed. Before long, she had written pages. Bertha was excited. She read what she had written aloud so I could get the full effect.

"I was right; you *do* have a flair for writing!"

"And you have a flair for encouraging. I couldn't have gotten started without you."

"Thank you. I guess we both tried something new today. Do you think next time I could stand on the soapbox?"

"Only if you're lecturing to the cat!"

Red Flag

It was seven o'clock on Saturday morning. Bertha and I were sitting on our favorite bench at the beach, enjoying the wind and the restless waves. There was a tropical storm brewing in the gulf, miles away, yet the surf already had a dangerous undertow. Red flags were flying, warning people to stay out of the water under penalty of law. The sky was overcast and ominous. At any moment, we could be running for the shelter of the car parked nearby.

We sat for a bit in silence with our eyes closed, listening to the thunderous waves crashing onto the seaweed strewn sand, the wind rushing past our faces, and the red flag flapping back and forth just behind us.

It was a truly delightful day and we were savoring every minute of it before the rain would send us home. After a bit, we started to talk about the weather, the beach, and the few people who were up and out already. Even though for us, it was a perfect day (we love the beach in all types of weather) most of the vacationers in town did not share our delight. It was Labor Day weekend—the last hurrah of the summer. It was the last weekend for self-respecting southern women to wear white shorts and shoes and carry white purses. Mother Nature was not cooperating with their plans for fun in the sun.

"Bertha, how upset do you think you would be if you had spent all this money and driven several hours to get to the beach only to find a sign saying you could go to jail if you got in the water?"

"Oh, not very." Bertha reached up to keep her lime-green, straw hat from blowing away. Even though it was windy, she wore it this morning with her lime-green spandex shorts and matching tank top. Of course, she had the lime-green flip-flops on too. As usual, she was styling.

"What do you mean, not very?" I was confused. "People come to the beach to play in the water and get a tan. It doesn't look like there will be much of either going on this weekend. How could you not be upset?"

"Well," Bertha smiled, "I wouldn't be upset because I would have set my intention for the trip...."

"Oh, I get it," I interrupted, "you'd set your intention that you wanted the red flags to come down and the sun to come out so you could have a glorious vacation."

"Actually," Bertha grabbed her hat back again from the frisky wind, "that's not at all what I would do."

"Then I'm really confused. What would your intention be?"

"I wouldn't wait until I got here to try to change the weather. I would set my intention as soon as I decided to come to the beach. My intention would be that I would want to have the best vacation ever. I would say that I wanted to sing and dance and laugh more than I ever had. I would say that I wanted to delight in everything I did on the trip. I'd even add that I wanted everyone around me to be having fun, too." Bertha adjusted her hat and continued. "I'd find just as many wonderful ways to express how good I wanted to feel on this trip as I could. Then once I got here, all I would have to do is sit back and let it happen."

"You are right, of course. I just never thought of it that way. I guess I thought that the only way to set an intention was to focus on exactly what you wanted and exactly how you wanted it to happen and that was that."

"Yes, I know. But there are some things like the weather that you can't control, so when you do it that way and it doesn't happen exactly like you wanted it to, then you are disappointed, and you close yourself off to your joy. That's why, for something like a vacation, I focus on how I want to feel, and then I am open to endless possibilities."

"So, what is your intention for today?"

"Oh, I want to see gorgeous things all around me. It's working, too." Bertha winked at me then looked at the muscular lifeguard who had just come on duty.

"O-o-o-h, I do like your intention. And you're right, the red flags don't seem to have interfered with it at all!"

We laughed as we ran for the car while dodging raindrops.

Up, Up and Away!

I was making my bed when I heard Bertha walk into the room. I turned to say hello and almost swallowed the pillow.

Bertha had on purple and white striped, skin-tight spandex riding pants tucked into red patent leather riding boots, and a bright yellow silk blouse peeping out of a traditional red riding jacket. She even had a little riding crop in her hand. Now I must say that in itself would be quite an outfit, but she also had on a lime-green aviator cap and goggles. Even for Bertha, this was an unusual look!

"Bertha, what are you doing?"

"Oh, I'm just about to leave. I'm going to be a balloon jockey. I thought you might join me. I wasn't sure exactly how a balloon jockey dressed so I came up with my own outfit: a combination of jockey and pilot. What do you think?" Bertha did a pirouette so I could get the full effect of her outlandish creation.

Now this answer required tact. I began with the easy part. "Bertha, what exactly is a balloon jockey and why have you decided to become one?"

"A balloon jockey flies a balloon." Bertha pointed to her aviator cap and jacket at the same time. "I decided to become one because Rita has been getting to me again with all that garbage she has to say."

"So?"

She twirled the riding crop as she spoke. "Well, there have been some other things that have been getting me down lately, too."

"That's interesting. I've been in a funk of sorts myself lately." I sat on the edge of the partially made bed. "I guess I was so low that I didn't even notice that you were too."

Bertha produced the soapbox and climbed aboard for a talk.

I couldn't help laughing out loud. "Oh Bertha, when you stand on the soapbox in that outfit, you look like the oddest lion tamer I have ever seen."

Bertha took a bow. "See? You're feeling better already!"

"Now that I'm smiling, why did you decide to become a balloon jockey?"

"I got to thinking that Mama used to say, 'Bertha Mae,' she always called me by my full name, 'Bertha Mae, things are going to happen in this life that you may not like. Now when they do, you'll have two choices. You can either sink down lower than a mole or you can rise above it. The choice is up to you.' You know, Mama was a very smart woman so I figured I have the same choices today. I can either sink down or rise above."

"I never realized that how I felt was my choice… until I met you. I just bumped along feeling like a victim a lot of the time. Maybe I should have spent more time listening to my Mama when I was young."

"We all have to find our own way in our own time. And today is our time. Let's rise above together! Can you think of a better way to get our vibrations higher than to fly in a hot air balloon?"

"Nope, it sounds like the perfect way to me. I'm definitely game to try it."

"I knew you would be."

I stood up to finish making the bed before we left. "Where will we get a balloon?"

Bertha hopped off the soapbox and tucked it into the corner, "Luckily, they are having balloon jockey classes at the community college this week. Now, what do you think of my outfit?" She pirouetted again.

I scratched my head and wondered how I could rise above that question and maintain a vibrational altitude.

Cele-Break

It was Saturday morning in early spring. I had planned a delightful day in the sun, in the dirt, in the garden. The rain had other plans.

I sat in my favorite over-stuffed chair. My feet were tucked snuggly under me. Staring at the rain splattered window, I was mesmerized by the seeming life of the raindrops clinging there. For the most part, they were tiny drops. As I watched, one would start to swell. It would get bigger and bigger and then, without warning, it would let go and streak down the window pane taking many unsuspecting drops along with it....

"You look like you're waiting for *The Cat in the Hat*." I turned my attention away from the window to the direction of Bertha's voice.

She strolled nonchalantly into the room.

I blinked and shook my head just a little to clear out any cobwebs lingering there from the night before and looked again.

Well, there had been no cobwebs and my eyes had not deceived me. Bertha was indeed dressed in a stunning lime-green, sequined ball gown. The slits up the side revealed a great deal of her long legs, and of course, her matching lime-green, high-heeled sandals. Her long red hair was in a classic French twist, topped off with a faux diamond and emerald tiara. Her favorite lime-green, ostrich feather boa slinked around her arms and hung down her sides.

My jaw must have dropped down to my knees. I swallowed hard. "Well, I don't think I could have been any more surprised."

I stretched my legs out and leaned forward. "Bertha, what are you doing?"

"I'm here for our Cele-Break." Bertha flipped her boa over her left shoulder for effect.

Getting up I headed toward the kitchen for another cup of coffee, thinking maybe that would wake me up. Maybe this was just a dream. I returned to find Bertha waiting for me. It wasn't a dream.

I blew on my coffee as I sat back down. "I can tell that you're itching to tell me what you're talking about and it's too early to play guessing games. Let's have it. What do you mean by our 'Cele-Break'?"

Bertha was indeed ready to explain. She pulled out the little soapbox she keeps tucked away for just such occasions. In that dress and those heels, I was afraid she would break her neck or maybe even put her eye out, as she stepped on the box. But as usual, Bertha managed with grace and ease.

She poised herself to speak. "A Cele-Break is a break from your day to celebrate your life."

Bertha paused to allow her words to sink in. "How do you like my party dress?"

"I love your dress, but I still don't understand exactly why you are wearing it at eight o'clock on a Saturday morning. Unless…you weren't out all night, were you?"

"No, I was not out all night, but I might be tonight. Who knows?" She tucked her chin down to her shoulder and looked coy.

"Whatever. Let's get back to the Cele-Break." I sipped my coffee and waited for the answer.

Bertha stood proudly on her soapbox. "Remember that television show called, *This is Your Life?*"

I nodded, "Yes."

"I used to love that show. All these obscure people would show up from the person's past and tell how this person had impacted their life in some way. Often the guest of honor was blown away by their comments. They never knew they were touching people's lives in this way." Bertha's eyes were sparkling. She was really getting into this.

"Yeah, I liked the show, too. Now what does that have to do with you standing on your soapbox on Saturday morning looking like Ginger from *Gilligan's Island?*" I leaned back in my chair and got comfortable; this could take a while.

"I always thought the neatest part of the show was how happy it made the guest of honor to hear all those nice things about themselves." Bertha smiled. "Do you really think I look like Ginger?"

I raised my eyebrows and tilted my head down, giving her "the look."

"Okay, whatever." Bertha shifted her weight on the soapbox. "Anyway, I thought that it would be wonderful to have that kind of experience…."

I jumped forward in my seat. "Bertha, are you going on television?"

"No, that's my point. The television show doesn't come on anymore." She stepped down from the soapbox and stretched her back.

"I've created a virtual *This is Your Life*. I call it *Cele-Break*. Do you want to play?" Bertha looked at me expectantly.

"Do I have a choice?"

"Not really," Bertha laughed, "just thought it would be polite to ask."

"What do I have to do?"

"Not much. Just go get dressed in something fun."

Reluctantly I headed to my room to change. I wasn't in the mood to play one of Bertha's games this morning.

Turning back to the den, I stated, "I don't want to change. If I'm going to play, it will have to be in my pj's."

Bertha's face lit up. "Oh that's perfect! Hurry up and sit down."

I returned to my chair and awaited Bertha's instructions.

"Okay, now close your eyes and we can start."

This time I obeyed Bertha's command and we were underway.

"Take a slow, deep breath. Now imagine. It's Saturday morning. You're sitting in your pj's enjoying a cup of coffee. The door bell rings. You open the door. There's a man standing there with a camera crew. They whisk you away to the TV station where you are the guest of honor on Cele-Break."

Bertha paused as I got the full picture in my mind. It seemed so real that I was a little embarrassed for not changing into something more appropriate for national television.

"They've just brought you on camera and told a little bit about you. In the background, we hear the first guest begin to talk about you."

I could feel the lights on the set. I even got butterflies as I waited to see who the first guest was.

"Now you tell me, who is the first guest?"

I didn't even hesitate to think. "My third-grade teacher. She's telling about the times that I gave my allowance to a classmate who never had money for a snack during recess and how that touched her deeply."

"Oh, that's great! Who's next?"

One by one I blurted out people from my past that I hadn't thought about in years. I was amazed that I had been unaware how I had touched their lives until now.

It was a delightful game. I had so much fun that I forgot about the garden and the rain.

Next it was Bertha's turn. She had quite a line-up, including women we had never even met whose lives had been transformed by her book, *Putting Your Best Foot Forward: A Woman's Guide to Life and Shoes.*

I laughed and slinked Bertha's boa on over my jammies. "Bertha, this was so much fun. I never thought that much about how I impacted other people every day. I feel great about me! How did you come up with the idea?"

"Oh, it was just an idea. It doesn't really matter what the idea is." Bertha sank down onto the sofa. "The main thing is to remember that life should be like a cup of Maxwell House Coffee."

I scrunched my face. "What?"

"Oh, you remember…Good to the Last Drop!"

Love Letter

Bertha was sitting at the computer typing furiously. There was a stack of dollar bills lying beside her and she was dressed in lime-green from head to toe. I mean – lime-green, strappy high-heeled sandals, lime-green spandex shorts and halter, and even lime-green reading glasses. She was quite a sight. She had even gone with shocking chartreuse nail polish!

Although I sometimes question my own sanity for doing so, I had to ask, "Bertha, what are you doing?"

"I'm writing a love letter." Bertha smiled as she looked up to answer.

Now I was intrigued. "A love letter? That's wonderful. Who's your new man?" I asked in rather rapid succession.

"You don't understand. There's no man."

I must admit I really didn't understand. "Okay Bertha, if there's no man, then who are you writing to?"

"Well, I'm writing to this stack of money." Bertha pointed at the obvious. "You know, I love money. I love to spend it. I love to share it. I even love to give it away. I especially love receiving money—lots of money. I love money that comes in the mail, money I earn, money I find in the street, money gifts, winning the lottery, essentially money from anywhere and everywhere—as long as it's legal of course. I love money. So I thought if I really love money, then I should treat it special and that's when I decided to write it a love letter."

"That's certainly a new concept for me. How did you come about this idea?" I peered over her shoulder.

Bertha lovingly touched her stack of money then looked at me with that Bertha twinkle in her eyes. "Well, you know one of the concepts in Law of Attraction is appreciation and a grateful attitude. Recently I realized that for years, I've not treated my money right."

I pulled up a chair and sat down next to her. "Exactly how have you mistreated money? Can you even do that?"

Bertha pulled the soapbox out from under the desk and climbed aboard. "I've been afraid there wouldn't be enough of it and I've even been embarrassed by it when I had a lot of it. I've been too shy to say 'I love money.' I have even bemoaned being broke when I had money sitting in the bank just waiting on me to decide how to spend it just because other people were complaining about not having enough."

"That sounds just like me," I interrupted her. "I thought that's how I was supposed to act. They always said that it wasn't polite to actually be proud of having money."

Bertha rolled her eyes. "*They* said a lot of things that aren't really helpful when it comes to living the life you want. *They* are more interested in their own needs than yours."

"Are you sure?"

"Absolutely! In fact, anytime I start a sentence with, '*they say,*' I make a point to stop and ask myself, 'What do *I* say?' That's what I listen to." Bertha pointed towards her heart.

"What do you say about money now?"

Bertha puffed out her chest and looked just as pleased as any new daddy at the nursery window. "I love money and I'm proud of it! I'm writing my money a love letter so it will know how much I appreciate it and all the things it does for me, like paying for new shoes and manicures. I dressed in green in honor of all money everywhere." Bertha extended her arms wide, open expressing the magnitude of her statement.

I pointed to the computer. "Do you mind if I use it when you finish? I think I may just write a letter of my own."

"That's a great idea!" Bertha stepped down from the soapbox and patted her stack of money lovingly. "Unless I miss my guess, this money will be inviting its friends over soon."

"What friends?"

"Oh, you know, Mr. Franklin, Mr. Jackson, Mr. Washington...."

"A-h-h-h, *those* friends; speaking of which, I came in here to bring your mail. Were you expecting what looks like a tax refund check?"

Bertha smiled knowingly and took the envelope.

Derby Girl

It was about 8:00 p.m. when I got home from doing errands. I was ready to kick back with a diet coke and a good movie, but then I saw Bertha and everything changed. She was coming from her room, obviously dressed for going out. The sixty-four-thousand-dollar question was where could she be going at this time of night (or at any time for that matter) dressed like that? Bertha was all decked out in a racing suit. You know the ones like NASCAR drivers wear, only hers was lime-green with "Shoe Mart" splattered across the front in flamingo pink letters. She had matching gloves and helmet in one hand and her car keys in the other. She was such a sight that even though I was afraid of the answer, I had to ask, "Bertha, what are you doing?"

"Well, I would think it is obvious," Bertha replied, flipping her hands in that "ta-da" way she had. "I'm about to drive in the demolition derby."

"The DEMOLITION DERBY?" I screamed in disbelief "Why are you driving in the demolition derby? What if you get hurt or killed or break a nail? What about your car? Are you driving your T-Bird?" I kept firing off questions so fast that Bertha didn't have time to answer until I finally took a breath.

"Oh, you are such a worrier," Bertha started to explain. "Actually, this is a challenge derby between me and Bruce."

"Bruce? Who is Bruce? Why would a Bruce challenge you?" I asked, getting even more confused.

"You remember Bruce. He's related on Grandma Minnie Mae's side. You know, he's the one who always seems to be carrying the weight of the world on his shoulders. I know I must have told you about him." Bertha sat down her helmet and gloves as she spoke.

I racked my brain and still couldn't place Bruce. I must have had a blank look on my face because Bertha continued without waiting for a response. "Oh, it really doesn't matter if you remember him or not. That's not the important part anyway. The important part is that he is in town for a visit and we met for lunch. I really didn't want to go, but you know how Grandma Minnie Mae was about our kin, so I accepted, even though he makes me crazy some times. He is so uptight and stiff...."

"Bertha, it still doesn't make any sense to me. Why are you challenging Bruce to a demolition derby just because he has a rather rigid personality? Again, let me remind you, that you might break a nail and you just got a manicure this morning." I threw this part in hoping to settle her down just a bit.

"I know. My nails do look nice. Isn't this a lovely shade? It's called 'Midnight Madness' because it creates such a stir, but that's beside the point. My nails will be just fine,"

Bertha smiled in a confident way and then became more serious. "When Bruce and I were having lunch I was talking about all the wonderful things going on in my life. I told him I always strive to feel good because I know that feeling good and appreciating are the best ways to allow more good things to come into your life. Well, Bruce just sat there stiff as a brick. It was like he was frozen or something. He said that he thought that was a bunch of hooey and that he didn't believe in such nonsense. He said he was man enough to shoulder what ever came up in his life, no matter how much it hurt, and that he didn't need any 'feeling good' or 'appreciating' to help him out."

Bertha stopped for a moment to let all of that sink in. It was hard to believe that this Bruce was any relation to Bertha with that kind of stiff attitude. "Oh Bertha, what happened then?" I asked, getting really curious.

"Well, you know I had to come up with some way to help him. Grandma Minnie Mae would roll over in her grave if I let him continue to think like that. So I really thought about a way to knock some sense in him so to speak and demolition derby is what came to mind." Bertha continued, "That's the way we used to settle things when we were kids, so I figured it was still the best way."

"You drove demolition derby when you were a kid? I can't believe your mama let you do that. Where did you get all the cars? Didn't you ever get hurt? Di...." I was getting out of breath and welcomed Bertha's interruption.

"Oh silly, of course we didn't get hurt or demolish any cars or whatever else you were about to conjure up in that wild imagination of yours," Bertha answered, laughing at the images she knew were running through my mind. "We did demolition derby down at the bumper car track. We were perfectly safe. But the one who got the other one cornered was the winner. I was the all-time champion then and I intend to win tonight, too!"

"You mean to tell me that you are going to drive bumper cars down at the track?" I clarified, not believing my ears.

"Yep, that's right. Wanna come watch?" Bertha invited, picking up her gloves and helmet.

"Of course I do. I wouldn't miss it!" I gathered up my purse and totally forgot about the movie I had wanted to watch earlier.

In no time, we were cruising down the road in Bertha's '56 T-Bird. I was relieved to know that it was safe. We pulled into our parking space just in time to see Bruce getting out of his truck. I recognized him right away. He had that stiff walk of a 'good ole boy' who could handle anything or anyone. His saunter said he was definitely ready for a good fight on a Saturday night. We joined him at the ticket counter where he and Bertha stared each other down as they bought their tickets. I made my way to the spectator section quickly so I wouldn't miss a thing. The cars at this track were made to look like different kinds of animals. There were only two left and Bertha made a beeline to the black cat car, leaving Bruce to fold his long legs into a little gray mouse car. I laughed under my breath, but Bruce didn't look any too amused.

And so the games were underway. Bertha took the first blow as Bruce drove straight into her, hitting her broadside and scooting her across the track. Bertha wasn't threatened in the least, and she gave her "cat" the gas and headed back in Bruce's direction. The competition was really heating up! This time she made the hit head on. The mouse went into a tailspin and quickly spun into a corner. Bruce looked a little disoriented as he was frantically turning the wheel in an attempt to set himself straight. Bertha moved quicker than lightening and the cat was bearing down on the defenseless mouse. She showed no mercy as she expertly pinned Bruce into a corner he couldn't get out of. Obviously, Bertha had won, but I had no idea what would happen next.

Bertha took off her helmet and smirked directly at Bruce. Bruce tucked his head in the agony of defeat and began to mumble something under his breath.

"Louder Bruce, I can't hear you," Bertha proclaimed, never dropping her stare.

"Okay, okay." Bruce held his head up and almost spit out these words: "Nothing is more important than that I feel good. I appreciate everything in my life. It's okay to ask for and accept help when I need it." The amazing part was that the more he spoke, the higher he held his head and the more his face softened. He actually looked like he meant what he was saying as he finished. "I don't have to carry the world around on my shoulders anymore."

"Not bad for a little game of cat and mouse!" Bertha exclaimed, as she slipped off her gloves and waved her still perfectly manicured nails as a symbol of her victory.

Stopping Over

The sun was just starting to stream into the kitchen window and dance on the fig tree and on Bertha. Yes, Bertha. It was 6:30 in the morning. Bertha was sitting at the kitchen table painting her nails 'flaming tangerine,' which was her favorite shade this month. Last month it was 'shocking chartreuse' and it was shocking I might add! So at least she had toned down a bit.

I poured myself a cup of coffee. "Bertha, what are you doing?"

Bertha looked up and over her reading glasses, smiling knowingly. "I'm stopping."

"I'm glad to see that doesn't mean stopping to wear your reading glasses. I thought we were never going to get the shocking chartreuse off the cat last time."

"It's not my fault that your cat is so nosey. It had no business sticking its tail between me and my nail polish. I can't help it that my eyesight isn't as good as it once was. Besides, I thought green was a good look for it!" She shook her hand back and forth to speed up the drying process.

"Whatever…thank you for wearing your glasses. So what are you stopping? It obviously isn't cat bashing." I blew on my coffee to cool it a bit.

"I'm stopping over." She removed her glasses and looked up at me.

The cat sniffed the glasses on the table and blasted out of the room like it had been shot from cannon. There was no doubt that it remembered the "shocking chartreuse" incident.

I sat down at the table. "Stopping over where?"

"Not where, what." Bertha touched up her pinkie.

"What? That makes about as much sense as—I can't even think of an analogy it makes so little sense."

"Then I'll be happy to explain." Bertha put the brush back in the bottle. "You have been saying for years that you are 'over.' You know, over worked, over weight, over tired, over loving, over giving, over reacting, and even over worried."

"Well, it's true."

"Just because it's true doesn't mean you have to talk about it and give your attention to it. That just brings more 'over' into your experience. There are a lot of things that are true about you that don't have anything to do with 'over'."

"You're starting to make sense. Go on."

"I decided today was the day to stop 'over.' Your reality may still be the same for a while. You may still be working long hours and weigh more than you want to, but with your focus on more positive things, you'll find that you're enjoying life more. Then pretty soon the 'overs' will be over."

"When you put it that way, 'stopping over' does sound like a good idea. I'm ready. Let's stop!"

"I knew you'd want to. That's why I got up early and put on my best lime-green dress and these adorable matching high-heeled sandals and decided to paint my nails. Now if you don't mind, I have nails to finish."

I looked down at those lime-green sandals and could tell that the polish on her toenails was still wet. With all certainty I knew that she had painted her toenails with the sandals on and that she had only painted the four nails on each foot that were showing. The little piggies were still chartreuse. I laughed to myself, "Only Bertha!"

Bertha was oblivious to my thoughts. She was already painting her nails again. The cat watched from the other room. Evidently it had stopped being overly curious about nail painting!

Ant Bed

Bertha and I were on an adventure. We were in New Mexico. Quite a long way away from home for southern girls, I might add. But Bertha had wanted to see the mountains and Bertha usually gets what she wants.

I was grateful to come along and keep her company. Truth be known, I love the mountains just as much as the beach, so it was a welcome change of pace.

On this particular day, we had hiked up a mountain trail a ways and were sitting on a big flat rock by the edge of a stream. The weather was perfect, not hot or cold. The sun was bright and yet there was plenty of shade. Bertha was all decked out in her hiking clothes. Of course they were as unique as Bertha herself. She had decided to blend in with our surroundings and chose lime-green head to toe. She started with her favorite lime-green straw hat and then added a lime-green shirt and overalls. She had even found the first pair of lime-green hiking boots I had ever seen. Amazingly, with the sunlight dancing through the leaves, she blended in perfectly. If not for the tufts of red hair straggling out from under her hat, she might have been invisible.

We sat there for quite some time just enjoying the serenity of it all. The calls of the birds making plans for later, the sound of the breeze rustling through the leaves, and the way the sunlight felt on our faces and arms, were truly a spiritual experience.

"Bertha, what are you thinking?"

"I'm not really thinking about anything in particular." Bertha closed her eyes and tilted her face upwards to fully face the sun and gentle breeze. "I suppose I'm just basking in the splendor of all of this. I'm just feeling good."

I watched a leaf floating in the stream for a moment, then I asked what was on my mind. "Bertha, there's something I don't quite understand about feeling good. You're always talking about feeling good being the most important thing and how you always choose what feels good. I don't mean to sound rude, but isn't that self-indulgent?"

Bertha opened her eyes and looked at me. "Give me an example."

"Well," I chose my words carefully. "Say I want to go to the beach on Thursday, it's a beautiful day after several days of rain.

Going to the beach would feel wonderful. Watching the dogs run and jump in the waves makes my heart sing. So if I am just going by what feels good, then I'll call into work and say that I am sick."

Bertha brushed a stray red curl back under her hat. "How would you feel if you did that?"

"I'd feel like I had lied. I would be afraid that I might get fired if I got caught. I'd feel selfish that my co-workers had to work harder while I was at the beach."

"How would you feel if you went to work instead?"

I scrunched my face in thought. "I'd be bummed a bit because I really wanted to go to the beach. But I'd be proud that I was honoring my obligation. I might even try to get off a little early if we weren't too busy so I could go after work."

Bertha gave me a confident smile. "So which choice would feel better?"

"Going to work. Who would have ever guessed I would choose work over the beach?"

"I knew you would. I knew when you looked at things a little deeper, you would understand that feeling good comes from a place of integrity, not from spur of the moment pleasure seeking. When your conscience is screaming '*DON'T*' chances are that action won't give you a good feeling in the long run."

I was amazed. "Bertha, how did you get so smart?"

"It's not that I'm so smart; it's just that I have learned how to choose things and thoughts that make me feel good. I really believe that nothing is more important than feeling good." She slid her hands across the rock and leaned back to continue her basking.

About that time, an ant crawled onto Bertha's hand and took a taste. "Ouch!" squealed Bertha.

"Well Bertha," I asked, slightly amused by the timing of Bertha's words and her unfortunate nibble, "if all that matters is that you feel good, what do you do when something happens that doesn't feel good… like the ant just biting you?"

"Oh, that's easy." Bertha shook her hand in the air. "I take my hand out of the ant bed and put it somewhere else."

And so she did.

Gravy

Bertha was listening to the pigeons cooing and the chorus of other birds chirping as she was sitting with her writing. A motor, possibly a lawn mower, was humming in the distance and car tires were crunching a gravel driveway like Rice Krispies in a bowl. It was peaceful, melodic, mesmerizing. The gentle breeze was tickling the spindly branches of a nearby tree as the sunlight peeked in and out of the clover, changing the color from her favorite lime to a deep forest green.

Bertha was "sitting with her writing" because it just wasn't coming at the moment. She had already completed two chapters of her book, *Putting Your Best Foot Forward: A Woman's Guide to Life and Shoes*, *Power Pump*, and *How to Dump the Heel When It's Over*. Now she was in the middle of her latest chapter titled, *Rhinestones: From Boardroom to Bedroom*, and although she knew the concepts she wanted to share, the words just weren't connecting.

Bertha knew this was okay. She knew that sitting quietly while the words gestated was the thing to do. She knew they would come. Bertha had even dressed for inspiration in her rhinestone-studded, black, high-heeled sandals, skinny black capris with the pink tube top and pink, floppy sun hat. She had her iced tea in a goblet with a flamingo stem and she was patiently waiting for the words to flow.

I was sitting across the courtyard writing my own thoughts and enjoying the peace and quiet.

Suddenly, we were surrounded by another tour group. Now we had been at this historic mountain lodge all week so we felt smug and possessive, like the place belonged to us. These tour groups interrupted our writing and were quite annoying.

I looked up just as Rita spied Bertha. That's right, Rita was amongst the tourists. You could tell right away that she was a tourist. She had double socks on with her un-scuffed hiking boots. Her skinny, black, strappy tee shirt was just skimming the top of khaki walking shorts with the pockets on the sides and she had a denim shirt tied around her waist. She had been taking pictures, and her disposable Fuji camera, dangled from her wrist like a gaudy charm bracelet.

I wondered what she was doing here. I know we didn't invite her. It's like she had a sixth sense that let her know when Bertha was doing something important and she would make a beeline to sabotage her. Today was no different.

"Oh Bertha," she screeched in that voice of hers, "what are you doing?"

Bertha looked up, none too pleased to see Rita invade our mountain retreat. "I'm here for the Taos Writer's Spa. I'm working on a book."

"You, a book?" snorted Rita. "Let me see what you're writing now."

Bertha slumped down in her chair just a bit. Rita was as pesky as a tick on a dog—sinking its teeth in, and growing fatter by the minute. Bertha reluctantly held up her morning's blank pages.

Rita didn't miss the opportunity to really tie into this one. "Why Bertha, you haven't written a thing. You call yourself a writer. You came all this way and paid all this money to be a writer. Don't you think the least you could do is write?"

Somehow, Bertha jolted back to the reality of who she was and her confidence quickly re-centered. Maybe she remembered that she had indeed written two wonderful chapters already and that the group had raved over them during sharing time, or maybe it was the words Rita said. I don't know what happened inside her head, but I have never been as proud of her as I was at that moment when in a deliberate drawl she said, "Rita, actually the least I can do is nothing. Everything else is gravy. There are some biscuits in the kitchen if you'd like to dip one in it."

She picked up her pen and tried to keep up with the words as they flowed onto the paper.

Wrong Number

Rita was feeling pretty smug. She had waited, maybe not patiently, but she had waited. Bertha had taken those earplugs out and could hear again. Just the opportunity Rita had been hoping and planning for.

She knew exactly how to get to Bertha and so she did.

The minute Bertha took out the earplugs, Rita started whispering ever so softly, "Bertha, you can't have it. You'll never have it. Why are you even trying?"

Rita's voice was so faint that Bertha wasn't even sure she was hearing anything. She didn't bother to put the earplugs back in. She just kept going about her business: getting her hair done and shopping for shoes. Every so often, she'd catch a whiff of, "Don't, Can't, Won't, Why," drifting in the breeze.

The words had a rhythm to them and they lulled Bertha. Although she wasn't aware of it at the time, she played them over and over in her mind like a TV commercial jingle. The more the words lulled her, the more they dulled her as well.

Before long, Bertha wasn't shopping for shoes as often. Some days she was even padding around the house barefoot. One day she wore the baby blue, snap front housedress that her Aunt Gladys had, misguidedly, given her last Christmas. Worst of all, she was considering getting all that gorgeous red hair cut off. It was just too much trouble. Bertha was so low on the vibration scale that if she had been a radio station, her call letters would have been YTRY.

The lower Bertha's vibration got, the louder Rita's words became. "See! Look at you. What have you got to show for yourself?" The voice grew louder. "Did you ever really think you could be successful? Did you really believe you were attractive? How much debt do you really have?"

Bertha began to feel physically ill. Her head hurt. She was dizzy. She was fatigued. She began to overeat and under exercise.

This may sound like a long, drawn-out process, but it took place over about a week's time. It was as though Bertha had gone from riding the tallest roller coaster with her arms in the air and that red hair flying in the wind, to sitting on a park bench barefoot, in a duster, feeding the pigeons day old bread and afterwards, going home and making a sandwich with the leftovers.

The Bertha I knew was quickly fading out of existence. "Bertha, what are you doing?" I asked gently.

Bertha sighed. "Nothing, what's the use?" She went to her room to take another nap.

Rita, on the other hand. was feeling great. Her sneak attack was working beautifully. By starting her "doubt campaign" softly and slowly, Bertha didn't even notice it, so there had been no need for a defense.

Rita was a mastermind all right, a sheer genius, smarter than Lex Luther even! Oh, she was feeling smug.

Bertha was vibrating lower and lower. Her nails were broken and the polish chipped. It didn't look good for the old girl. She was even starting to look like an old girl!

I wanted to help her, to snap her out of it, but I understood that she would have to do that herself. Thanks to the lessons that Bertha had taught me, I knew that she was the only one who could make things better for her. So I did the best thing I could for her, I kept myself in a good emotional place and I held good thoughts about Bertha. I thought about how she always found a way to feel good; how this was only a temporary situation; and how she always came out of a slump even more focused and ready to enjoy life to the fullest.

One day I came home and found Bertha sitting at the kitchen table just staring at a single rose in a little bud vase. She had a hint of a smile on her face. I thought for a moment that she was catatonic or something.

"Bertha, what are you doing?" I dropped my packages on the counter.

"Oh hi, I didn't hear you come in. I was just appreciating this rose." Bertha pointed to the bud vase. "Look how beautiful it is. It's called Brigadoon. I love the creamy white and coral of the petals."

That was the first positive thing I had heard her say in a couple of days, so I left her to her appreciation.

The next morning I noticed her bed was made, and she was sitting at the kitchen table admiring her rose and doing her nails.

Rita was getting a bit concerned. Even though she was cranking up the volume, Bertha had started to vibrate on a bit higher level again. In desperation, Rita was yelling at the top of her lungs, "**Don't! Can't! Won't! Why!**"

Bertha didn't hear her. She was walking on the beach with the dogs and the sound of the waves was drowning Rita out. Bertha even picked up a starfish or two as she walked. When she got home, she rearranged the pink flamingos in the front yard and cut a bouquet of zinnias for her room. "You are so beautiful," I heard her telling them as she arranged them in a bright yellow vase. She turned on her favorite CD and swirled around the room holding her bouquet like a dance partner. She was smiling.

Rita kept screaming louder and louder, but Bertha couldn't hear her over the laughter in her own heart.

That night, Bertha came out dressed to the nines. She had on a black and white polka dot halter dress fitted at the waist with a black patent leather belt. Bertha wore brand new black patent leather high heel sandals and carried a wide-brimmed white straw hat with a black band and bow. She had on "Stop 'Em in Their Tracks" red lipstick and nail polish. I must say she looked stunning.

"Bertha, where are you going?"

"Oh, I have a date. We're going to ride the roller coaster and then we're going dancing." She twirled around so I could get the full effect. That outfit certainly was made for dancing.

"Have a great time!" I called as she walked out the door.

Shortly after Bertha left, the phone rang. A very hoarse voice said, "Don't, Can't, Won't, Why."

"I'm sorry, you must have the wrong number." I hung up the phone.

Happy "Berthaday"

Bertha was sitting at the desk busily writing when I got home from the bakery with her birthday cake. Yes, it was her birthday or "Berthaday" as she loved to call it. Bertha had long since given up telling how old she was. When I asked her, she just smiled coyly and said, "Maturity-something." So I didn't ask anymore. What's age anyway?

Bertha was all decked out in honor of her day. She had on lime-green capris and a lime-green tube top. Of course, she had on the matching high-heel sandals and nail polish. Since this was a celebration, she had added a lime-green pointed birthday hat to her "Berthaday" outfit. There was even one of those little blow out horns lying on the desk beside her journal. She was definitely in the birthday mode.

"Bertha, what are you doing?" I asked, as I set the cake on the kitchen table.

"Oh, I'm making my journal entry for next year's Berthaday. I can't wait to see what kind of cake you got. Hold it up so I can see it," she said.

I held the cake up. It was the perfect cake for Bertha. Essentially, it was a traditional favorite white cake with white icing, but the decorations made it all Bertha. The top was covered in lime-green icing to look like grass and there were lots of pink, plastic flamingos positioned all around the cake instead of candles. Of course, it said, "Happy Berthaday!" Her smile proved that she loved my surprise.

As I lowered the cake gently back onto the table, I asked, "Bertha, exactly how do you make a journal entry for your next birthday?"

"Well," she explained, "I know that my experience comes from what I really want and believe that I can have. So at first, I really thought about what I wanted in this coming year. When I got really clear about it, I started writing in my journal for next year about how it all happened and how wonderful it was when it happened. I wrote about how I felt, what I was wearing (of course) and who I was with … all just like it had already happened. When I write the details, I start to feel just as excited as if it has already happened, and the more excited I become, the more I start to believe that it can happen. The more I actually believe it can happen, the more I want it, and the more I want it, the more excited I become and the momentum just keeps building and then it actually starts to happen."

Bertha paused to catch her breath. She was getting excited just talking about it. Her face was radiant as she spoke.

The ringing of the doorbell interrupted us. When Bertha got up to answer the door, I glanced down at her journal entry. It began, "Last year was the most perfect Berthaday ever. I had a flamingo cake and I got the most exquisite flowers...." I looked up as Bertha entered the room carrying the most exquisite flowers I had ever seen!

Tourist

"So Bertha, what are you doing today?" I poured another cup of coffee to enjoy with my morning crossword.

"Oh, I think I'll go to the beach and play tourist."

Bertha's reply took me so off guard that I almost spilled my coffee as I turned to speak. "Just exactly how do you play tourist and why would you want to? You can go to the beach anytime – you live here."

"Well, I know I can go anytime and I do go often. I just rush down there and walk or maybe lie on a towel for a while."

Bertha grabbed the soapbox out of the corner and climbed aboard. The commotion woke the cat from its morning nap. It must have thought the topic was the wayward hairball found earlier in Bertha's bathroom, because it skedaddled from the room.

"That cat is rude. First hairballs, now interrupting my speech!"

"It's probably trying to tell you something," I laughed. "Now tell me more about going to the beach and playing tourist."

"It's just that the beach is so easy for me to get to, I don't really appreciate it like I would if I were a tourist. As a tourist, I can ask people questions about the area, like where the best places to eat are and what's fun to do. If I go as a local, everyone thinks I should already know everything. Help me remember to bring the camera." Bertha pointed to her beach bag.

I sipped my coffee and listened.

"I also get to explore all the neat new shops and stuff like that. You'd be surprised at all the things you never notice when you don't take the time to really look at where you are. When I go as a local, I'm just in a hurry to get there and get home. As a tourist, it's like a mini-vacation for the day."

"It is true that we are in a rut of just going to the same places and doing the same things over and over. I can't remember the last time we even tried a new restaurant. I keep thinking that I'd like to go on a trip because I'm bored—and I'm not even exploring here!"

"That's it exactly! I'm going to rent one of those loungers that come with the umbrella and the kid to move it every time the sun shifts. I'm taking some music and cold water and I'm spending the day. Wanna come?" Bertha didn't wait for an answer; she hopped off the soapbox and hurried to her room to change.

She soon returned in her favorite purple bikini and lime-green cover up. Of course she had the matching straw hat and flip-flops and those funny pointed sun reader glasses. As usual, Bertha was styling. I had even squeezed into my conservative black one-piece and decided to join her. Playing tourist sounded like fun.

Lottery

We had no more than finished Saturday dinner when Bertha jumped up and started rushing around clearing the table and loading the dishwater. I was quite amazed. Bertha was usually more difficult than the kids had been when it came to kitchen duty. So what was up? Curiosity got the better of me.

"Bertha, what are you doing?" I carried my plate to the sink and started to rinse it off.

"Oh, I'm hurrying to get the kitchen clean," Bertha answered, almost out of breath from all the rushing around.

"Yes, I see that Bertha, but why are you in such a hurry?"

"Well, I want to go get my lottery ticket before tonight's drawing." Bertha barely stopped long enough to answer.

A lottery ticket? So that explained the way she was dressed. Every time Bertha had anything to do with money, she wore lime-green. She said the color attracted money to her. So anyway, that explained the lime-green capris and the lime-green top with pink flamingos and a few choice sequins here and there. Of course, she had on matching pink high-heeled sandals, and she had gone back to the shocking chartreuse nail polish. I'm really glad she hadn't found matching lipstick yet. Instead, she had settled for the perfect shade of pink to match her cute flamingo dangling earrings. (Did I mention that the pink flamingo is the symbol for the Florida lottery?) Yes, Bertha was ready to attract a lottery prize that night.

"Oh," I sighed. "I'm so unlucky. I never win the lottery."

"Really? Unlucky?" Bertha dried her hands. "When exactly is the last time you bought a lottery ticket?"

"Well, let me see. Maybe about five years ago I bought one."

"Okay, let me get this straight. You bought a lottery ticket five years ago and you can't figure out why you never win the lottery. Is that right?" Bertha looked quite serious.

"Yes, that's right. I'm just not lucky." I shook my head in dismay as I closed the dishwasher door.

Bertha made that little "humph" sound and turned to me. "It's not that you aren't lucky. It's just that you don't have a chance."

"Well isn't that the same thing?"

"Oh, not at all." Bertha rubbed lotion on her hands. "You don't have a chance because you don't have a ticket! You know they have conducted some pretty impressive studies and found that 100%, that's 100%, of the people who won the lottery nationwide had a ticket."

Quick as a wink I slipped into something green and we were cruising down the road in Bertha's Thunderbird.

I painted my nails on the way!

I Spy

It was Saturday morning and I had slept in. Bertha was already in the den drinking coffee and reading the newspaper. A little odd for her because she generally chooses to make her own news rather than read about others' misfortunes. So I was a bit surprised, but not nearly as much as when she put the paper down.

She was sitting in her favorite chair already fully dressed; at least I hoped she was. All I could see were those black high-heeled sandals with the rhinestones and an oversized black trench coat. Her red hair was pulled up and under a man's black felt hat. I had the fleeting thought that she might be going to flash someone! If that thought was concern, then I quickly escalated to panic when I noticed a similar hat and coat lying across the arm of my chair!

"Bertha, what are you doing?"

"It's not what *I'm* doing; it's what *we're* doing," she replied, eyes twinkling. "I'll explain after you get dressed."

I was actually relieved as I went to dress. That indicated that Bertha was dressed under that trench coat! I pulled on shorts and sandals then returned to the den.

"Now, put on your hat and coat and I'll tell you what we're doing." Bertha pointed towards my chair. This was all very mysterious so I quickly did as I was told.

"Okay, I'm ready." I buttoned up my coat. "Now tell me."

"Remember when we were kids and we used to play 'I Spy'? Well, we're going to play my grown-up version of it today. The object of this 'I Spy,' is to spot as many things as you can that you like or that make you happy. Then you point them out. It's simple. Come on, let's go!"

Jumping into Bertha's pink '56 Thunderbird with the top down, we took off. Soon Bertha pointed to a beautiful house on the beach. "I Spy a fantastic beach house. Look at that view!"

Shortly it was my turn. "I Spy the Florida Lottery pink flamingo!" I giggled remembering the first time Bertha got me to buy a lottery ticket.

Bertha was next as we drove by a florist. "I Spy a dozen red roses. I do love getting roses from my special man."

And so we spent the day "spying." We went everywhere. We spied everything: from yachts to toasters, from songs on the radio to couples holding hands, from handsome men to snazzy cars. Of course, Bertha spied lots of shoes, some of which came home with her and one pair even came home with me!

It was a glorious day. We spied so many things that pleased us and that we would love to have in our lives, but mostly we laughed and chatted and had a perfectly delightful time.

We were still laughing as Bertha slowed the car and turned into the driveway.

"Bertha, I've had so much fun that I'm almost disappointed to be home. I loved spying things that make me happy. What a wonderful game."

"There's one thing that I didn't tell you about the game."

"Really, what?"

"I didn't tell you that when you spy things that make you happy and you take time to appreciate them that more and more things will come to you that will make you even happier. And then you'll be happier and then you'll notice even *more* happy things and then you'll be happier. It's like a delicious cycle."

"Then I'm about to overflow with things that make happy, 'cause I'm in a great mood."

Bertha put the T-bird in park and took out the keys. I looked over to the right and noticed that the gardenia was in full bloom. I hadn't even noticed it before we left. Getting out of the car, I went straight for the bush. I picked a couple of blossoms for the vase in my room. It was amazing. Their fragrance immediately took me back to a special prom corsage. It was as if I was actually surrounded by giggling high school girls dressed in chiffon and lace. I could see my date's face – we were so in love. I felt like that giddy school girl again. What a wonderful memory.

"Bertha look! The gardenia bloomed."

She didn't even look surprised. "I Spy...."

Tuned In

Something very strange was going on. Bertha had the feather duster in her hand and was happily dusting the den. This could have seemed normal except that Bertha usually didn't dust. She said dust bunnies have rights, too! It was Saturday morning about ten o'clock. I had been outside tending my roses and had just come in for a drink when I saw her.

Bertha was dressed in her favorite purple spandex shorts with the flamingo pink halter-top and of course pink high-heeled sandals. That part was normal, or at least expected!

It was the fact that she had on earphones: the kind that should have been attached to a cassette player, except that they weren't. That was odd. The little wire was just dangling in the breeze so to speak.

She was acting strange, even for Bertha.

I was curious. "Bertha, what are you doing?"

Bertha didn't respond. She just kept dusting and sort of swaying like she was listening to music or something. But she wasn't connected to anything. I walked over and touched her on the arm.

Bertha was startled and took off the earphones. "I didn't hear you come in."

"Well, I can tell that," I laughed. "Bertha, what are you doing?"

"Oh, I'm listening while I dust." Bertha gave the feather duster a shake to demonstrate her point.

"But Bertha, the earphones aren't connected to anything." I pointed to the dangling cord. "What are you listening to? And more importantly, what possessed you to dust?"

"Well, if you must know and I know you must, I might as well do this right." Bertha put down the feather duster and climbed on the soapbox.

The cat immediately went to sniff what it thought might be a chicken dinner, but the smell of dusted bunnies sent it sneezing into the other room.

Bertha rolled her eyes. "I'm not even going to comment on the cat today."

"Just as well. It doesn't usually seem to help any." I sat down to hear her out.

"I'm listening to my inner voice." Bertha pointed to the earphones that now were dangling around her neck. "I have found that I can tune in to my inner voice and really hear what it has to say when I tune out everything else."

"What kinds of things does your inner voice say?"

"It can say almost anything depending on what's on my mind. Some people would call it talking to myself or maybe even daydreaming. Basically I'm thinking about what I want and how things are showing up in my life. I'm just getting quiet enough that I can hear what I have to say."

"Interesting. That sounds a lot like what I'm doing in the garden with the roses. But what I don't understand is, why are you dusting?"

"As long as I was listening to my inner voice, I thought I might as well get rid of a few cob webs, too." That said, she smiled, stepped off the soapbox, put on her earphones, and quickly tuned back into the "Bertha Station."

I had gotten so involved that I was back outside before I remembered I was thirsty. This time I just went to the water hose!

Monkey Grass

Bertha was in the front yard in the tiny spot that we call the "garden." It was only about five square feet, but it was ours. We had planted roses that morning, a deep pink "Mr. Lincoln" and a delightful "Yellow Dream." Both were sure to give us many bouquets of fragrant blossoms soon. Having decided to take a break, I was fanning myself in the shade, sipping on a glass of iced tea.

As always, Bertha was all decked out for the task, complete with purple leather gardening gloves, lime-green sneakers with lemon-yellow socks, and a tangerine jump suit. Her long red hair was peeking out from under a grape straw hat. Bright pink cat lady sunglasses protected her eyes from the sun's glare. Bertha was more colorful than the flowers!

She was getting ready to spread some pine straw and plant some bright pink geraniums in pots, but what happened next took me by surprise. She started to pull up clumps of monkey grass.

"Bertha, are you doing?" I tilted my head to get a better look.

"I'm pulling up the monkey grass of course." Bertha stood up and arched her back.

This was puzzling. "But why? It's perfectly good monkey grass."

"Well, for starters," Bertha brushed back a stray red curl, "it takes away from our lovely new rose bushes and for another thing, I don't like monkey grass very much. Never did."

"But Bertha," I reasoned, "it came with the house. It's perfectly good monkey grass. You can't just pull it up and throw it away. That stuff costs money."

"Not only can I...I just did!" Bertha gave a tug at a particularly well-planted monkey. "When are you going to understand that just because something is there, we don't have to accept it and keep it? If we don't like it, we can let it go.

"The monkey grass was crowding out the roses and geraniums." Bertha swept her hand in the direction of her new plants. "It made things look cluttered. It was too much of something we didn't want and not enough of something we do want. Does that make sense to you?"

"Not really. I was raised with that 'waste not want not' philosophy. So it seems to me that we may be wanting soon."

Bertha grabbed her soapbox out from under a rose bush and climbed aboard. "Oh, we all were, but it just doesn't make sense when you think about it. What is having monkey grass choking out our roses and geraniums going to keep us from wanting later? Is it like we'll never want new clothes or a new car or whatever because we have an abundance of monkey grass?"

Bertha paused to take a breath. I covered my face with my fan so that she couldn't see me snicker. She continued. "And if I get rid of this monkey grass, will we suddenly enter some black hole of wanting? Will they make a movie about the women who wanted too much because they wasted monkey grass?"

I couldn't help it, I laughed out loud at how ridiculous it all sounded when Bertha explained it. I placed my fan in my lap. "You have made a believer out of me. Dig away, but do we have to throw it out?"

"I'm way ahead of you." Bertha jumped down from her perch and quickly placed three little monkeys in a box and sat it on the curb. The attached sign read, "Free to a good home."

It wasn't long before a neighbor drove by and stopped for the monkey grass. "Thanks Bertha!" she waved, "I've really been wanting some monkey grass just like this."

Bertha waved as she drove away. "See? it's like Grandma Minnie Mae always said, 'A place for everything and everything in its place.' The monkey grass has a place—it just isn't at our house!"

I surveyed our lovely garden. "I couldn't agree with you more, but now that it's gone, I really want a new yacht...." I ducked quickly to avoid Bertha's garden gloves whizzing through the air.

Combat

I came in through the garage door weighted down with groceries, thinking perhaps Bertha would help me unload the rest from the car and put them away. I sometimes forgot that I was dealing with Bertha, and that nothing was ever as I might imagine it would be. Today was certainly no exception.

Bertha was seated at the kitchen table dressed all in camouflage. I was even more startled by her appearance when she turned around. Bertha's face was painted camouflage, too. If not for the AWOL red curls sneaking out of the military-style cap she was wearing, she would have totally blended in with the fig tree. Just then, I looked down and noticed the camouflage high-heels. Definitely not military issue by my accounts, but they fit Bertha just fine. There were colored markers and bits of paper lying on the table next to a large slingshot.

I must say I was curious so I had to ask, "Bertha, what are you doing?"

Bertha smiled. At least her teeth were still white. She grew more serious as she answered, "I'm going to war."

"Oh Bertha, no!" I started to protest, and then continued frantically "Did something happen while I was at the store? Did the President declare war? Aren't you too old to be drafted? Did they recall the draft? Can you march in those shoes? *Why* did they give you a slingshot instead of a gun? You'll be killed, or at least put your eye out!" Thankfully Bertha interrupted me because I was getting out of breath.

"Calm down," Bertha reassured me. "It's not that kind of war." Relieved, I set the groceries on the cabinet and sank into the chair next to her.

"Then what kind of war is this, exactly? Does it involve the cat?" I asked, remembering what I thought had been idle threats made earlier this morning.

"No, it doesn't involve the cat either. Although, it has been a bit pesky lately," laughed Bertha. "Give me a second and I'll explain." Bertha continued as she folded one of the pieces of paper and shot it into the air with the slingshot.

"Okay now," continued Bertha, "you know I firmly believe that what I focus on and think about is what comes into my life, even if it's not what I want."

"Yes, of course I know that," I said in that "duh" tone of voice. "Who could live with you and not know that? Now what has that got to do with the Army clothes and slinging spit balls at the plants?"

"First of all, they're not spit balls," explained Bertha. "They are PMMs. That stands for Positive Message Missiles." It was then that I noticed a whole pile of "missiles" were already in the corner.

"Now I'm really confused, and the ice cream is melting." I grunted as I got up and started to put the groceries away.

"It's quite simple. For some time now, I've been sending out positive intentions and focusing on what I want. It is working, too. I have noticed positive changes in many areas of my life. Then suddenly, when I least expect it, a little negative bomb lands right at my feet and blows me away for a few days. This really had me perplexed. How was this happening? I am in a positive place. Why were these little negative bombs attacking me out of the blue? Were my thoughts attracting them?"

Bertha really had my attention now. I had noticed the same thing happening in my life and just assumed that I was more negative than I thought. I closed the freezer and returned to the table.

Bertha continued. "Then I finally figured it out just this morning. Those little negative or 'stink' bombs as I call them, are left over from all those years of negative thinking. I must have stock piled a bunch of them and just haven't had time to get rid of them yet. That's why I'm launching PMMs. I'm blowing up the stockpiles and I'm attacking the ones that are already headed this way before they hit the ground. Essentially, I'm flooding the air with positive messages."

"Oh Bertha, this is a very important war," I replied. "What kind of positive messages are you sending?"

Bertha responded as she flung another PMM towards the corner making that "P-K-Q-UU" noise little boys make when they pretend to blow things up. "Things like I want to feel good. I want to be healthy. I want to be prosperous. I want to spend time with harmonious people. You know, the usual. I'm just deliberately sending lots and lots of them. What do you think?"

"I think you're really on to something. In fact, I'll even make some of my own." I wrote, "I want to feel joy in everything I do", carefully folded it, and thumped it like one of those paper footballs we used to make as kids. "P-K-Q-UU!"

Puzzled

I came home from work and found Bertha sitting at the kitchen table sorting through a huge stack of old photographs.

"Bertha, what are you doing?"

"Oh. Hi. I'm going through all these old photos to see where I've been." Bertha swept her hand across the table.

"Bertha I don't understand. Why would you have to look at photographs to know where you've been? You were there. Can't you remember? Is that it? Have you lost your memory?" I was getting very concerned. "Do you need to see a doctor? Do you need to lie down?"

"Oh no, no," chuckled Bertha. "I'm not losing my memory and I don't need a doctor, unless he is cute and single, and I really don't want to lie down right now."

I sat down in an empty chair. Between all this excitement and a busy day at work, I was confused and exhausted. Maybe *I* needed to lie down.

Bertha must have sensed my confusion because she climbed aboard her favorite soapbox. In her best instructive voice she continued, "I was contemplating my life, where I want to be, what I want to do, and I realized that my life is a joining together of a lot of individual pieces of experience. All these pieces fit together like a puzzle...."

"Would that be a 500 or 1000-piece puzzle?"

"Very funny!"

"Sorry, I couldn't resist. By all means, please continue."

The cat jumped into the middle of the table scattering the pictures. Undaunted, it sniffed a few and jumped down again, and went on about its business as if it had never gotten up there in the first place.

"That cat is always trying to get all up in the middle of my business." Bertha pointed at the pesky feline.

"It was just "puzzled" about our conversation."

"Cute. Anyway, I was comparing my life to one time when I was putting this really big puzzle together. I had all these pieces scattered all over the table. I knew immediately where some of them, like the four corners went, then there were some that I sort of figured out because of color or shape, but there was one or two that made no sense at all. I couldn't even tell if they belonged in that puzzle box or not. I started to throw them away because they seemed so out of place that I knew they couldn't fit in my puzzle, but after a time, when I got more of the pieces in place, those odd balls started to make sense."

"I've been around you for a while now and I think there have been quite a few odd balls in your life."

Bertha shot me that look like Mama used to when I needed to settle down in Church on Sunday morning. I got the message: no words needed.

"Back to my analogy, it's the same way with life experiences. Sometimes something happens that makes no sense at all. I may even think it is a bad experience, but when I look back and see all the pieces, I realize that it was actually a perfect fit."

"You mean like my unfortunate second marriage? It seemed like a complete failure and waste of time, but when I look back on it I see that I learned many valuable things about myself, things that I would never have learned if I hadn't had the experience." I adjusted the pictures lying in front of me to avoid making eye contact.

"That's exactly what I mean. I should have given you the look sooner!" Bertha laughed, as she stepped off the soapbox and scooted it back into the corner.

She sat back in front of her pictures. "All of that made me want to look at my puzzle thus far, and what better way than looking at these old photographs? I'm glad I did, because I had forgotten a lot of things from my past. Things I'm sure at the time I thought I would remember forever."

Bertha pointed to an old black and white photo. "Look at this one of Grandma Minnie Mae and me. She would die if she knew her slip was showing. Oh and look, here is Mama and me on my first birthday. She was so pretty all dressed up." Bertha was almost bubbling over each photo in turn.

I noticed a small picture lying face down to one side and reached to pick it up. On the back was written, "Bertha's first day of school." I turned it over. I would have known Bertha anywhere... even without the caption. There she stood with all that red curly hair pulled back with a yellow satin ribbon that matched her stiffly starched, yellow organdy dress. She had on white ruffled socks (and panties too, I'm sure.) She had on those sparkly plastic dress-up high-heeled sandals. They were exactly the kind I had always envied at the toy store, only to have my mama tell me, "No...you'll break your neck!"

I held up the photo for Bertha to see. "It's easy to see that this 'piece' belongs in your puzzle!"

"Book 'Em Bertha"

I got up early and found a fresh pot of coffee in the kitchen. I was grateful that Bertha must have gotten up first and all I had to do was pour and enjoy. This was definitely my kind of day. I fed the cat and made my way to the den.

"Good morning Bertha. What are you doing?"

"I was just sitting here enjoying my coffee and remembering a dream I had last night. It was one of those that seem so real. 'Wanna hear it?"

I got cozy in my favorite chair with a light-weight lime-green chenille throw. The cat jumped on my lap as if on cue. "Does it involve the cat?"

"No, no, this wasn't a nightmare!" Bertha shot the cat a nasty look and it shot one right back. Good to see the "cold war" was still on even in the midst of summer.

"Good. Then I'm game. Let's hear it."

Bertha put her coffee down and grabbed the soapbox from the corner. "It was so cool. You and I were in a new television show."

I leaned forward. "This sounds good already. Go on."

"In the beginning of the show, the screen is dark and a deep voice says, 'In the World of Universal Laws, One Law Rules Supreme: The Law of Attraction.' Then the screen lights up and pans to us dressed in these police uniforms except they're lime-green and flamingo pink, of course. We're part of the Attraction Squad."

I took a sip of coffee. "Sounds to me like you've been watching that police show again."

"Well, maybe. But listen to what happens next." Bertha was so excited that she was almost bouncing on the soapbox. "The plot went something like this—we were assigned to go all over the city and look for people who were down and out and help them to live a better life."

I patted the cat. "Definitely sounds different than most police shows."

"Oh, it really was. On this 'episode,' we found this woman who was just a mess. She was leaving her husband, and her kids were on drugs, and she was in bad debt, and her pedicure was way overdue! So you went up to her and said, 'Ma'am, your life is in shambles.

We're taking you into custody. Bertha, read her her rights.' That's when I came over and read her the Bertha Rights."

"I thought they were Miranda Rights."

"Not in my dream! So I read her the Bertha Rights. 'You have the right to create your own reality. If you do not deliberately create the life of your dreams by choosing good-feeling thoughts, then one will be created for you by your own negative thoughts and emotions. You have the right live the most fabulous life you can imagine. If you focus your energy in a positive way, everything you desire in the universe can and will be provided for you'."

"Hey, that's pretty interesting. What happened next?"

"I don't know. I woke up. But it got me thinking that I could create a wonderful TV show. I'll call it *Book 'Em Bertha*. What do you think?"

"You have the right to create your own reality…."

Bullfrog

The sun sparkled on the South Carolina marsh. Bertha and I were on an adventure and had gone for an early morning drive. We had stopped at a boat launch and were sitting in her Thunderbird enjoying the quite Sunday morning.

I had a lot on my mind. I had been considering a career change for some time now. I knew that I wanted to be a full-time writer. ever since Bertha and I had started writing. I had known that this was my passion, but never until now did I conceive of it being a viable option.

It was the "viable option" that had me a tad bit terrorized. Lately, the thought of selling the house and living on the equity just wouldn't let me alone. In all honesty, it had never been an option before. Property values on the Gulf Coast had only just sky rocketed in the last six months. Suddenly I had equity; I had options.

The sound of Bertha opening her car door interrupted my thoughts. "Bertha, what are you doing?"

"Oh, I thought I'd go sit on that bench over there. It's such a lovely morning that I wanted to get the full effect."

"It is beautiful here. I think I'll join you. There's something I've wanted to talk to you about anyway."

We sat in silence for a few minutes just breathing in the beauty of it all. Bertha turned to me. "So, what's on your mind?"

"I'm considering quitting my job, selling the house, and living on the equity so that I can write full time. We'll live in a little rental house. It will probably mean leaving the coast," I blurted out quickly. "Now, I've said it and you can go ahead and tell me I'm crazy!"

"I don't think you're crazy."

"You don't?"

"Of course not. How do you feel when you think about writing?"

"I get so excited. I love to write. I love the way the words flow onto the page. I love to watch the faces of people as they read what I have written and see their expressions change as the words settle in with them. I love knowing that I have that ability. I love knowing that I can touch lives in a positive way with my writing." I could feel my excitement growing just talking about it.

"How do you feel when you think about your current job?"

"Well," I scrunched my face in thought, "it pays pretty well. I like the people that I work with. As jobs go, it's a pretty good one. I've had a lot worse."

"From the difference in the energy you have when you discuss writing and work, I'd say you've already made the decision. Now it's time to take the bullfrog by the horns and do it."

"Are you sure it isn't taking the bull by the horns?"

Bertha headed to the trunk of the car, returned with her soapbox, and climbed aboard. "Oh no, that implies taking some kind of rash action. Even though your decision may seem abrupt to some people, I know that there is nothing rash about it."

"How do you know that?"

"That's pretty easy. Your face lights up like a kid in a toy shop every time you mention writing, for starters. We've talked about how good you feel when you write. I know you've been focusing positive energy in that direction."

"That's all true. But what does it mean to take a bullfrog by the horns?"

"Taking the bullfrog by the horns is how I describe the action you take after you've dreamed about something and thought it through until it no longer seems unreasonable to you. In fact, it seems like the next logical step."

"You know, it does sound logical to me now. That's what has been scaring me!"

"You're gonna be just fine." Bertha hopped off the soapbox and took it back to the trunk. She was carrying a big net when she returned.

"Now what are you up to?"

"Oh, you are so excited about the possibility of writing that I figured we'd better catch you a bullfrog before you croaked!"

I Choose

Bertha had a suitcase under one arm and her lime-green straw hat with a nosegay of yellow flowers under the other. She was dressed in her favorite purple spandex shorts, the ones with the sparkle in them, and a fuchsia halter-top. It was almost enough "bright" to give me a migraine.

"Bertha, what are you doing?"

"I get to choose and I choose to move on," Bertha waved her hat in the air, "to move up, to expand."

I eyed her critically. "Not much room to expand in those shorts."

Bertha ignored my unsolicited fashion critique.

"I choose to create," she continued. "I'm creating more and this just isn't the place I'm willing to stay in anymore."

"But Bertha, we've been so comfortable here. We can manage here. We're getting by here."

Bertha would have no part of it. "I get to choose and I choose to move on."

"What if you're wrong? What if there isn't more out there? What if you lose what you already have? What if you end up living under a bridge, eating out of a garbage can? What if the other homeless people don't like you? What if you can't even find a decent bridge to live under?" I was getting frantic.

Bertha smiled. In what could have been a tender moment, she reached out, body slammed me into the wall, and started out the door.

"Bertha," I stumbled after her.

Bertha just kept walking. "I get to choose and I choose to move on." She threw her stuff into her 1956 Thunderbird convertible.

I barely had time to jump in the passenger's side before we were off. I turned around to take one last look at the house. That's when I noticed that Bertha had written, "I chose" on the trunk with shoe polish.

And so she did. And so did I. And moving day was over.

Empty Nest

The phone message from my coach Michele, intrigued me. "Help! My daughter moved out this weekend. My nest is empty. What do I do?"

Total switch. She was seeking *my* advice!

I suppose it wasn't too shocking. With her encouragement, I had started writing a book for women in predicaments just like hers. It was a collection of thought-provoking exercises designed to re-ignite the passionate flame in a woman's life, or some such drivel.

The only problem was that the book wasn't flowing. I felt more like a Brownie Scout rubbing damp sticks together in a vain attempt to earn a merit badge than an up-and-coming author.

I dialed her number more to commiserate than actually offer sound advice. Evidently she had flown the coop, along with her daughter, and I got the machine. For whatever reason, I decided to e-mail her rather than leave a message.

Michele,

Name your empty nest. I know that sounds crazy, but give it a try. Many people name their cars and even their private body parts, so why not name your empty nest?

Once you name your empty nest, give "her" a personality. Sit down and write a paragraph describing her. Is she grumpy? Lively? Sexy? Lazy? Lonely? Funny? Have some fun with this. There isn't a right or wrong answer. This is yours.

Mine is Bertha, actually Bertha Butts. She was the largest of the Butts sisters and also the most vocal. So my nest is Bertha. I like that name. My nest is Bertha!

The best part of doing this is that once you have named your empty nest and given her a personality, she becomes almost like a person and therefore is someone that you can change and create anyway you want.

It's more fun to say, "Okay Bertha, we're going to spruce you up a bit. I think a luscious coat of coral paint would really do wonders for you. What do you think?" Rather than to say, "This place is a dump.

The walls are drab. I really have to paint them. Maybe I'll get around to it next month."

Do you feel the energy shift?

When I talk directly to Bertha, there is a positive energy. It is fun to offer her a new "coat"- a little like buying a new dress. When I bemoan the fact that my house is drab and dull, my energy is also drab and dull and it is quite apparent that next month the walls will continue to be drab! On the other hand, Bertha is going to bug me until I get her that new coat.

It's also more fun to think of going home to Bertha than to think of going home to an empty house.

Bertha becomes a virtual friend. Everything I do for Bertha, is like doing it for someone who appreciates it.

Bertha also is supportive and nurturing. When I come home tired and cold, Bertha keeps the rain off and turns on the heat.

WOW! I like Bertha more every minute.

All of this shifts the feeling from one of resentment of coming home to no children, to coming home to an adventure and a friend. I personally like the shift!

Give it a try and let me know how it works.

I smiled as I clicked "send" and the e-mail was on its way.

Later, Michele and I had a good laugh about Bertha. What a great chapter for the book. "Name That Nest" had a Dr. Seuss rhythm to it that pleased me. Those damp sticks I'd been rubbing together were starting to smoke!

Although I thought I was well on the way to earning my literary merit badge, unlike a good scout, I was in no way prepared for what happened next!

Author's Note:

My intention in writing this book was to keep it vague enough so that any woman picking it up could see herself and her unique situation within the stories. In that respect, it is your book, not mine. Now that you have finished, I thought you might enjoy getting to know the characters that starred in the book from my perspective.

"I" represents me, you, and a little bit of every woman I have ever known. Not every story is my own; some were inspired by women asking, "How would Bertha deal with this?"

Although Bertha started as the name for my "empty nest" she soon revealed herself as the voice of wisdom I hear when I go within and listen quietly. My sister told my mother, "Jane is writing about her inner voice. She just gave it a name and a wardrobe!"

Rita amounts to my inner critic or nag that delights in doing the Mexican Hat Dance in my garden of freshly planted dreams. It was rather fun turning Bertha loose on her with a water hose.

Lizzy is the part of me that is so tiny she is almost invisible until she roars, "I want to be heard. I want to be known."

Mama stars as herself with a dash of your mama too!

Grandma Minnie Mae is a combination of the wisdom of my grandmother Linnie B., my friend's grandmother Minnie, and my own mother, Clara Mae.

Bruce is simply a medical condition known as, "Adhesive Capsulitis," A.K.A. frozen shoulder. When traditional medicine and therapy wasn't working, I thought Bertha should take him on. He is much better now!

Pepper stars as the cat and continues to delight in sitting in the middle of my work, my bed, and anywhere else that is in the way. The attitude is real. Truth is stranger than fiction!

Maybell, playing the part of shy dog, went to doggie heaven midway through the writing of the book after loosing a fight with a rattlesnake. Betsy followed a couple of years after. I miss them both. The beach was never the same without them.

Sneak Preview

"Becoming Bertha"

Home Again

The movers were waving as they prepared to leave the house. "Goodbye, Bertha. Hope y'all will be happy in the new house. And keep that cat in line…" could be heard over the sound of the motor as the truck pulled away from the curb.

Bertha returned their waves. "Don't worry—that cat's no match for me!" she exclaimed, before turning from the porch towards the door, disappearing into the maze of moving boxes and off-kilter furniture.

I wasn't quite ready to go back inside. The thought of blank walls and stacks of boxes sitting like soldiers awaiting orders, unsettled my stomach in a way that only moving can. I stood there a few more minutes taking it all in. Here I was, here *we* were, in a totally unfamiliar house, an unfamiliar place. Albeit my home town, it felt like I'd never been there.

A momentary sense of normalcy resumed as I heard Bertha on the other side of the door raising her voice to the cat. "Hey, you! Get away from that box!" She had stamped each of her boxes with a large flamingo so there would be no question as to whose stuff it was. And I might add that most of those boxes contained shoes—what else? "Those are *my* things. Now, shoo!"

I wasn't sure if the cat *shooed* or not, but I had my doubts. The two of them are usually doing their rendition of a Mexican standoff with no discernible winner, although each would say that they were. At least Bertha's relationship with the cat hadn't changed.

Moving had been Bertha's idea. She wanted to grow, to expand, to move on. Me? I was comfortable where I was. No, not necessarily deliriously happy, but familiar with my life. Content in my discontent, I suppose. Oh, I had come a long way since Bertha moved in with me a while back. My attitude was better. I had friends. I was doing things I enjoyed. With Bertha's encouragement, I had even started writing, and part of the purpose of this move, was to give me the time and space to write. I was making progress. But that was then. That was *there*. I felt like I'd left all that behind. Now here we were, back where I'd started in a way—back to this town and yet—a long way from home.

Bertha must have sensed my discontent because she joined me on the porch, carefully closing the door to contain the adventurous cat that resorted to peeking through the curtainless window. "What's up? You seem so melancholy."

"I don't think I'm melancholy. It's more like... reflective. It just hit me. I really don't know who I am here.... Here I've been a child, a mother, a wife. I'm not exactly any of those things now, and yet here I am. I guess I just don't know who I am or what I'm supposed to do with myself anymore. I'm not even sure about writing." Sighing, I sat down in a bright pink Adirondack chair. It was Bertha's of course.

Bertha's gaze scanned the porch obviously looking for a soapbox, returning to me when she found none. Naturally, the lack of a platform didn't keep her from telling me a thing or two. We are talking Bertha, after all. "Being *you* has nothing to do with a town or a house. It has only to do with you. It doesn't matter where you're living. It doesn't matter if you're with friends. It doesn't matter if you're at work. You really aren't a different person in different situations—in different places. Sure, you may act a little differently in different circumstances, but you are always the same person. It's time to figure out who you are and what you want. It's letting go of who you have been and becoming who you are. And as you *do* that... the writing will take care of itself. It always does." Her voice was calm and soothing, a bit out of character for Bertha, who was usually bouncier and bubblier and...well...bossier.

I stared at my feet. "I understand that it is time. I do want to figure it out. I just don't have a clue how to do it. I thought I was catching on before we left, but now that we're here I'm at a loss."

"I know you don't know. But you will. That's why you have me. That's what I came to show you, to teach you. We have made a start, but it was only a start."

Looking up at her, I cupped my hands above my eyes shading them from the afternoon sun. "I think I need remedial classes. I'm not sure I remember those lessons...."

Bertha interrupted, "Honey, you still have all the lessons that you've learned. They haven't gone anywhere. They're right here." She patted her heart with her right hand for effect.

"You really think I still have them?"

"Of course," she reassured me. "You can't unlearn something you've already learned. It's like Grandma Minnie Mae always said, 'You can't un-ring a bell.'" The chiming of a nearby church bell validated her point. She gave an appreciative look to the sky before continuing. "Besides, I've got lots of new things up my sleeve. I may even pull that cat of yours out of a hat…."

Hearing a loud thud, we both turned to the window just in time to see the cat disappear amongst the moving boxes. Evidently, it didn't want to be a part of Bertha's new tricks.

"Oh Bertha, I wish I were you. You always seem to know who you are and just the right thing to do."

Bertha smiled knowingly. "Grandma Minnie Mae always said to be careful what you wish for… you just might get it. Are you sure you'd want to be all of this?" She gave a shimmy—showing off her skintight periwinkle capris and matching tube top. Of course she had on matching high-heeled sandals. "Besides, you're a lot more like me than you know."

"Yeah, right! Don't think I'm gonna start wearing spandex and high-heels anytime soon," I smirked.

She looked at me like the proverbial cat that'd just swallowed the canary. I probably should have asked about it, but I had another matter on my mind. "Bertha, there's just one more thing. I'm a little scared."

"Of what?"

"Of whom I really am. What if I don't like myself?"

Tilting her head to the left, her mouth became a knowing smile. "Honey, you don't have anything to be afraid of. You are one special person…."

"You think?"

"I not only think, I know. And I'll bet that one day really soon—you're gonna know it, too." Reaching into an open box, she removed a large, pink, plastic bird and proceeded to stake it into the lawn.

"Bertha, what are you doing?"

"Duh, everyone knows—home is where the flamingo is." She gave it one more push for good measure.

We were home.

www.ingramcontent.com/pod-product-compliance
Lightning Source LLC
LaVergne TN
LVHW051601080426
835510LV00020B/3075